ISBN 978-0-266-00168-3
PIBN 10964401

This book is a reproduction of an important historical work. Forgotten Books uses state-of-the-art technology to digitally reconstruct the work, preserving the original format whilst repairing imperfections present in the aged copy. In rare cases, an imperfection in the original, such as a blemish or missing page, may be replicated in our edition. We do, however, repair the vast majority of imperfections successfully; any imperfections that remain are intentionally left to preserve the state of such historical works.

1 MONTH OF
FREE
READING

at

www.ForgottenBooks.com

By purchasing this book you are eligible for one month membership to ForgottenBooks.com, giving you unlimited access to our entire collection of over 1,000,000 titles via our web site and mobile apps.

To claim your free month visit:

www.forgottenbooks.com/free964401

English
Français
Deutsche
Italiano
Español
Português

www.forgottenbooks.com

Mythology Photography **Fiction**
Fishing Christianity **Art** Cooking
Essays Buddhism Freemasonry
Medicine **Biology** Music **Ancient
Egypt** Evolution Carpentry Physics
Dance Geology **Mathematics** Fitness
Shakespeare **Folklore** Yoga Marketing
Confidence Immortality Biographies
Poetry **Psychology** Witchcraft
Electronics Chemistry History **Law**
Accounting **Philosophy** Anthropology
Alchemy Drama Quantum Mechanics
Atheism Sexual Health **Ancient History**
Entrepreneurship Languages Sport
Paleontology Needlework Islam
Metaphysics Investment Archaeology
Parenting Statistics Criminology
Motivational

PUBLIC LAWS

OF THE

CONFEDERATE STATES OF AMERICA,

PASSED AT THE FIRST SESSION

OF THE

FIRST CONGRESS;

1862.

Carefully collated with the Originals at Richmond.

EDITED BY

JAMES M. MATTHEWS,

ATTORNEY AT LAW,

AND LAW CLERK IN THE DEPARTMENT OF JUSTICE.

TO BE CONTINUED ANNUALLY.

RICHMOND:

R. M. SMITH, PRINTER TO CONGRESS.

1862.

ADVERTISEMENT.

CONFEDERATE STATES OF AMERICA,
Department of Justice,
Richmond, June 1, 1862.

By an Act of the Provisional Congress, approved on the 5th day of August, 1861, section third, it was made, *inter alia,* "the duty of the Attorney General, at the close of each session of Congress, to cause all the laws and resolutions having the force of laws, and all treaties entered into by the Confederate States, to be published under the supervision of the Superintendent of Public Printing." This section was amended by a further act, approved on the 17th day of February, 1862, which provides, "That the third section of said act be so amended as to authorise the Attorney General to cause three thousand copies of the Provisional and Permanent Constitution, and of all the acts and resolutions and treaties of the Provisional Government of the Confederate States which are not secret, to be published in one volume, at the close of the present session of Congress, arranged, and with marginal notes, and indexed, as provided in said act." The effect of this amendment, it will be observed, is to repeal the third section of the first mentioned act, so far as it applies to the legislation of the Provisional Congress, and restrict its application to the laws and resolutions passed by Congress under the Permanent Constitution, and to treaties entered into by the Confederate States under that Constitution.

For sometime after the passage of the act of the 5th day of August last, it was impossible to comply with its requirements because of the fact that the requisite paper—"paper equal in quality to the edition of the laws of the United States, as annually published by Little & Brown,"—could not be procured; and it was not 'till very recently that the Superintendent of Public Printing succeeded in obtaining it. For this reason the laws and resolutions have been published, heretofore, under special resolutions of Congress, for temporary convenience, on paper of inferior quality, and without regard to the provisions of the act. This is the first publication that has been made in conformity with its provisions.

The following laws and resolutions have been carefully compared with the original Rolls on file in this Department, and all typographical errors other than those noted in the table of errata, corrected. Where anything essential to complete the sense is omitted in the Rolls it is inserted in the text, included in brackets.

JAMES M. MATTHEWS,
Law Clerk.

LIST

PUBLIC ACTS AND RESOLUTIONS

OF CONGRESS.

𝔄cts of the 𝔉irst ℭongress of the ℭonfederate 𝔖tates.

STATUTE I.—1862.

LIST OF THE PUBLIC ACTS OF CONGRESS.

ERRATA.

Page.	Ch.	Sect.	Line.	
29,	28,	1,	2,	After the word " Secretary," read " of the Treasury.
33,	34,	2,	2,	For " or " read " of."

PUBLIC ACTS OF THE FIRST CONGRESS

OF THE

CONFEDERATE STATES,

Passed at the first session, which was begun and held at the City of Richmond, in the State of Virginia, on Tuesday, the eighteenth day of February, A. D., 1862, and ended on Monday, the twenty-first day of April, A. D., 1862.

JEFFERSON DAVIS, President. ALEXANDER H: STEPHENS, Vice-President, and President of the Senate. THOMAS S. BOCOCK, Speaker of the House of Representatives.

CHAP. I.—*An Act supplementary to An Act entitled "An Act to establish the War Department," approved February twenty-first, eighteen hundred and sixty-one.* — Feb. 27, 1862.

The Congress of the Confederate States of America do enact, That if any officer of the army be appointed Secretary of War, and enter upon the duties of that office, he shall not thereby lose his rank in the army, but only the pay and allowance thereof, during the time he is Secretary of War, and receiving the salary of that officer. — *Army officer, appointed Secretary of War, not to lose his rank.*

APPROVED Feb. 27, 1862.

CHAP. II.—*An Act to authorize the suspension of the writ of habeas corpus in certain cases.* — Feb. 27, 1862.

The Congress of the Confederate States of America do enact, That during the present invasion of the Confederate States; the President shall have power to suspend the privilege of the writ of *habeas corpus* in such cities, towns and military districts as shall, in his judgment, be in such danger of attack by the enemy as to require the declaration of martial law for their effective defence. — *Suspension of the writ of habeas corpus.*

APPROVED Feb. 27, 1862.

CHAP. III.—*An Act to increase the Clerical Force of the War Department.* — March 14, 1862.

The Congress of the Confederate States of America do enact, That there be added to the number of clerks now authorized by law in the War Department, twenty additional clerks, to be divided among the — *Clerical force increased in the War Department.*

Compensation.

several Bureaus, in such proportion as the Secretary of War may deem most advantageous, to receive compensation as follows, to-wit : Six at the rate of fifteen hundred dollars per annum ; six at the rate of twelve hundred dollars per annum, and eight at the rate of one thousand dollars per annum.

APPROVED March 14, 1862.

March 14, 1862.

CHAP. IV.—*An Act to amend An Act entitled An Act in relation to Public Printing, approved February twenty-seventh, eighteen hundred and sixty-one.*

Act of 1861' Feb'y 27, amended.

Advertising proposals for carrying the mail, in additional number of papers.

The Congress of the Confederate States of America do enact, That the eleventh section of the act of the Provisional Congress, entitled "An Act in relation to public printing," adopted the twenty-seventh day of February, eighteen hundred and sixty-one, be, and the same is hereby, so amended as to authorise the Postmaster-General, when, in his opinion, sufficient notice will not be given of advertisements for carrying the mail, by inserting such advertisements in three newspapers in each State, to advertise such proposals in such additional number of papers as may be necessary to give them full publicity : *Provided, that,* by so doing, no greater expense be incurred than if said advertisements be inserted in but three newspapers.

APPROVED March 14, 1862.

March 17, 1862.

CHAP. V.—*An Act to regulate the destruction of property under military necessity, and to provide for the indemnity thereof*

Destruction of cotton, tobacco or other property, authorized.

The Congress of the Confederate States of Ameaica do enact, That the military authorities of the Confederate Army are hereby authorized and directed to destroy cotton, tobacco, military and naval stores, or other property of any kind whatever, which may aid the enemy in the prosecution of the war, when necessary to prevent the same, or any part thereof, from falling into the hands of the enemy.

Perpetuation of the testimony of such destruction according to act of 1861, Aug. 30).

SEC. 2. *Be it further enacted,* That the owners of property destroyed under the operation of this Act, as well as those persons who shall voluntarily destroy their property to prevent the same from falling into the hands of the enemy, are hereby authorized to perpetuate the testimony of such destruction, in the manner prescribed by an Act of the Provisional Congress, entitled "An Act to perpetuate testimony in cases of slaves abducted or harbored by the enemy, and of other property seized, wasted or destroyed by them," approved thirtieth August, eighteen hundred and sixty-one ; and such owners and persons shall be entitled to indemnity out of the proceeds of property sequestered and confiscated under the laws of the Confederate States, in such manner as Congress may hereafter provide.

Indemnity to owners out of Sequestration fund.

APPROVED March 17, 1862.

March 24, 1862.

CHAP. VI.—*An Act to regulate the compensation of the Officers of the Senate and of the House of Representatives.*

Salary of the Secretary of Senate.

The Congress of the Confederate States of America do enact, That the Secretary of the Senate shall receive an annual salary of twenty-five hundred dollars, payable monthly. That the Secretary of the

Senate be allowed to appoint an assistant Secretary at a salary of two thousand dollars per annum, and two clerks at a salary of fifteen hundred dollars per annum, each, payable monthly. That the Sergeant-at-arms of the Senate, shall receive an annual salary of two thousand dollars; and the Doorkeeper of the Senate shall receive an annual salary of fifteen hundred dollars; and the Assistant Doorkeeper, shall receive an annual salary of twelve hundred dollars, all payable monthly; and the Page of the Senate, shall receive an allowance of two dollars per day, during the session of the Senate.

Secretary may appoint an Assistant Secretary and two Clerks. Their Salaries.

Salaries of Sergeant-at-arms, Doorkeepers and Page of the Senate.

Sec. 2. *Be it further enacted,* That the Clerk of the House of Representatives shall receive an annual salary of twenty-five hundred dollars, payable monthly. That the Clerk of the House of Representatives be allowed to appoint three assistants, at a salary of fifteen hundred dollars per annum, each, payable monthly. That the Doorkeeper of the House of Representatives receive an annual salary of two thousand dollars, and the assistant Doorkeeper shall receive an annual salary of twelve hundred dollars, payable monthly; and the Pages of the House of Representatives shall receive each, an allowance of two dollars per day, during the session of the House.

Salary of Clerk of House of Representatives.

Clerk may appoint three Assistants.—Their Salaries.

Salaries of Doorkeepers and Pages of the House.

Approved March 24, 1862.

The Congress of the Confederate States of America do enact, That the following post routes, upon which the service has been placed by the Postmaster General, be, and the same are hereby established, and his action, in putting the mail service upon the same, is hereby confirmed, to wit: A post route from Hernando, by Pleasant Hill, to Olive Branch in the State of Mississippi; also one from Waxahachie, by Alvarado and Buchanan, to Acton, in the State of Texas; also, from Goliad, by Cummengsville, Beeville and San Domingo, to Oakville, in said State of Texas; also, one from Sherman, by Chalybeate Springs, Dickenson, Delaware and Horse Shoe Bend, to Gainsville, all in the State of Texas; also, one from Dresden, by White Rock, Hillsboro and Covington, to Grand View, in said State of Texas.

Certain post routes established; and action of Postmaster General in putting mail service on same, confirmed.

Sec. 2. The following new routes are also hereby established, viz: one from Camden by Buffalo, to Miller's Bluff, in Ouachita county, in the State of Arkansas; also, one from Walnut Hill, in Lafayette county, in the State of Arkansas, by Spring Bank, Bright Star and Courtland, Cass county, Texas, to Havannah of the county and State last aforesaid; also, a post route in the State of Arkansas, from Washington, in Hempstead county, by Ozan Postoffice, Wilton Postoffice, on the Little Missouri river, Caddo Gap or Centreville Postoffice, Caddo Postoffice at Farr's Mill, McConnell's Mill, Goodner's, Hickey's, Waldron Postoffice, to Fort Smith, in Sebastian county; also, the following routes in the State of Georgia, to wit: from Valdosta, by R. P. Hutchinson's to Irwinville; also from Covington, by way of Oak Hill and McDonough to Jonesboro; also, a post route from Jonesborough, in the State of Tennessee, to Grassy Creek, in the State of North Carolina, crossing the Iron Mountain where the McDowell and Yancey turnpike road terminates.

Establishment of certain other post routes.

Approved March 24, 1862.

March 24, 862.　　CHAP. VIII.—*An Act to provide for the further defence of the Bay of Mobile, and the Alabama River.*

Appropriation for the defence of Mobile Bay and the Alabama river.

The Congress of the Confederate States of America do enact, That the sum of one million and two hundred thousand dollars is hereby appropriated for the further defence of the Bay of Mobile, and the Alabama river, to be expended, at the discretion of the President, by the Secretary of the Navy; and that the disbursement of said money shall be made in the manner provided by law for appropriations for the Navy.

President may raise a corps for service in said bay and river.

SEC. 2. *Be it further enacted*, That the President is hereby authorized to raise a corps for the temporary and special service provided for in the first section of this act in the Bay of Mobile, and the Alabama river, consisting of a number of men not exceeding six thousand, and of such commissioned and non-commissioned officers, and of such rank as the President may deem necessary, who shall severally receive such pay and allowances as he may determine.

APPROVED March 24, 1862.

March 25, 1862.　　CHAP. IX.—*An Act to provide a staff and clerical force for any General who may be assigned by the President to duty at the seat of Government.*

The Congress of the Confederate States of America do enact, That whenever the President shall assign a General to duty at the seat of Government, the said General shall be entitled to the following staff,

Staff of General assigned to duty at seat of Government. Clerks.

to wit: A military Secretary, with the rank of Colonel; four aids-de-camps, with the rank of Major; and such clerks, not to exceed four

Pay and allowances.

in number, as the President shall, from time to time, authorize. The pay and allowance of the Military Secretary and aids-de-camp, shall be the same as those of officers of cavalry of like grade; and the salaries of the clerks shall not exceed twelve hundred dollars per annum

Offices, fuel, &c., to be provided.

for each. Such offices, office furniture, fuel and stationery, shall be provided for the said General as the duties of his office may render necessary, to be paid for out of the appropriation for the contingent expenses of the War Department.

APPROVED March 25, 1862.

March 25, 1862.　　CHAP. X.—*An Act to regulate the compensation of Members of Congress.*

Compensation and mileage of Senators, Representatives and Delegates in Congress.

The Congress of the Confederate States of America do enact, That the compensation of each Senator, Representative and Delegate in Congress shall be twenty-seven hundred and sixty dollars for each year, and mileage at the rate of twenty cents per mile for each session,

When receivable.

to be paid in manner following, to wit: On the first day of the first session of each Congress, or as soon thereafter as he may be in attendance and apply, each Senator, Representative and Delegate shall receive his mileage and all his compensation, from the beginning of his term, to be computed at the rate of two hundred and thirty dollars per month; and during the session, compensation at the same rate. And on the first day of the second or any subsequent session, he shall receive his mileage aforesaid and all compensation which has accrued during the adjournment at the rate aforesaid; and during said session

Proviso.

compensation at the same rate: *Provided*, no member shall receive mileage for more than two sessions of any Congress, unless more than twenty days shall elapse between the adjournment of one session and the beginning of another.

Sec. 2. That the President of the Senate *pro tempore*, when there shall be no Vice-President, or the Vice-President shall have become the President of the Confederate States, shall receive the compensation allowed by law for the Vice-President; and the Speaker of the House of Representatives shall receive double the compensation above provided for Representatives, payable at the times and in the manner above provided for payment of the compensation of Representatives. *When President of the Senate pro tempore to receive compensation allowed the Vice-President.*

Speaker of the House to receive double the pay allowed Representatives.

Sec. 3. That this law shall apply to the present Congress; and each Senator, Representative and Delegate shall be entitled to receive the difference only between their *per diem* compensation, already received under the law now in force, and the compensation provided by this act. *This law applicable to present Congress.*

Sec. 4. That it shall be the duty of the Committee on Pay and Mileage and the Secretary of the Senate, respectively, to deduct from the monthly payment of members, as herein provided for, the amount of his compensation for each day that such member shall be absent, without leave, from the Senate or House respectively, unless such Senator, Representative or Delegate shall assign as the reason for such absence the sickness of himself or of some member of his family. *Deduction for absence without leave.*

Approved March 25, 1862.

Chap. XI.—*An Act to regulate the mode of paying the members of the Senate and House of Representatives, and the disbursement of the contingent fund.*   March 26, 1862.

The Congress of the Confederate States of America do enact, That the compensation which shall be due by law to the members and officers of the Senate and House of Representatives of the Confederate States, shall be certified as follows, to-wit : That which shall be due to the members and officers of the Senate shall be certified by the President thereof, and that which shall be due to the members and officers of the House shall be certified by the Speaker thereof, and the same shall be passed as public accounts and paid out of the public treasury. *Compensation due to members and officers of two Houses of Congress; how to be certified.*

Sec. 2. All certificates granted by the President and Speaker, as aforesaid, of the amount of compensation due as aforesaid, shall be deemed, and are hereby declared, to be conclusive upon all the departments and officers of the Government of the Confederate States. *Certificates granted to be taken as conclusive.*

Sec. 3. All moneys which have been or which may be hereafter appropriated for the contingent expenses of the Senate and the House of Representatives, respectively, shall be paid at the Treasury from time to time, in such sums as the President of the Senate and the Speaker of the House may approve, on the requisition and draft of the Sergeant-at-arms of the Senate and the Clerk of the House, respectively, and shall be kept, disbursed and accounted for by them, respectively, according to law, who are hereby deemed and declared to be disbursing officers. *Payment of appropriations for contingent expenses of Congress.*

Who declared to be disbursing officers of said appropriations.

Sec. 4. The said Sergeant-at-arms and Clerk shall each, within ten days after the passage of this act, enter into bond, with one or more sureties each, to be approved by the Secretary of the Treasury, in the penal sum of five thousand dollars each, with condition for the faithful application and disbursement of such funds as may come into their hands, respectively, or may be drawn from the Treasury, under this *To give bond.*

Penalty.

Condition.

Where bonds to be deposited.

or any other act; which bonds shall be deposited in the Treasurer's office, and it shall be the duty of the Sergeant-at-arms and Clerk, here-

Disbursing-officers hereafter chosen likewise to give bond.

after chosen, to give bond as aforesaid, within ten days after his election and undertaking the duties thereof, and before he shall draw any draft or make any requisition as aforesaid.

Payments to be by drafts.

SEC. 5. All payments on account of the compensation due by law to the members and officers of the Senate and House of Representatives, respectively, shall be by drafts drawn by the Sergeant-at-arms of the Senate and the Clerk of the House, respectively, on the Treasurer, to be verified by the certificates of the President of the Senate and Speaker of the House aforesaid.

Disbursement of contingent funds subject to approval of committee of accounts.

SEC. 6. The disbursement of the contingent funds of the two Houses, hereby placed under the control of the said Sergeant-at-arms and Clerk, respectively, shall, before payment, be approved by the Committee of Accounts in each of said Houses respectively.

Estimates to be submitted, and disbursement to be in accordance with estimates.

SEC. 7. The said Sergeant-at-arms and Clerk shall regularly submit estimates to their respective Committees on Accounts, and no disbursement of the contingent funds of either House shall be audited by said committees, except in accordance with such estimates.

Tabular statements to be made by disbursing officers at the close of each session.

SEC. 8. The said Sergeant-at-arms and Clerk shall, as soon as practicable after the close of the present and each succeeding session, make up a tabular statement of all appropriations made during the session, and also a table or statement showing the names and compensation of the clerks and officers of each House, together with a detailed statement of the items of expenditure out of said contingent funds for the next immediately preceding session; in which statement the disbursements shall be arranged under the several heads of printing, stationery, and so on, until each and every head of expenditure has been specified and described, with the cost of every item; and which statement shall exhibit, also, the several sums drawn by the said Sergeant-at-arms and Clerk, respectively, from the Treasury, and the balances, if any, remaining in their hands. Said Sergeant-at-arms and Clerk

Statements to be printed, and sent to members of Congress

shall cause said statements to be printed and a copy thereof sent to each member of the Senate and House of Representatives, as soon as practicable.

APPROVED March 26, 1862.

March 28, 1862.

CHAP. XII.—*An Act to fix the times for holding the Confederate Court for the Northern District of Georgia.*

Time for holding Confederate court for Northern District of Georgia.

The Congress of the Confederate States of America do enact, That hereafter the Confederate Court for the Northern District of Georgia shall be held on the first Wednesday in the months of June and December in each year.

Laws repealed.

SEC. 2. That all laws conflicting with this act be, and the same are hereby, repealed.

APPROVED March 28, 1862.

April 2, 1862.

CHAP. XIII.—*An Act to enable the States assuming the payment of their quotas of the war tax, to pay the same into the Treasury.*

The Congress of the Confederate States of America do enact, That if any State which has agreed to assume the payment of her quota of the tax imposed by the act approved August 19th, 1861, entitled "An States assuming the payment of their Act to authorise the issue of Treasury Notes, and to provide a war tax quotas of the War for their redemption," shall not have been furnished with a correct Tax, to pay the probable amounts therecollated list of the taxes assessed on the people of such State before of into the Treasury. the first day of April, 1862, the Secretary of the Treasury shall agree with the Governor of such State upon the probable amount of such assessment, and the State shall be entitled to pay the same, less ten per centum, in like manner, and with like effect, as if such payment had been made before the said first day of April: *Provided, however,* That when the corrected assessment is made out, such State shall pay Proviso. to the Confederate Government or receive therefrom, as the case may be, the deficiency or excess of the correct amount due from her on the assessment, allowing to the State the deduction of ten per centum on the deficiency, if any.

Approved April 2, 1862.

CHAP. XIV.—*An Act to authorise the President to increase his personal staff.* April 2, 1862.

The Congress of the Confederate States of America do enact, That Additional aids-de-camp allowed the during the existing war the President may, as Commander-in-chief of President Their the forces, appoint, at his discretion, for his personal staff, four aids- rank, pay and allowde-camp, in addition to the number now allowed by law, with the rank, ances. pay and allowances of a colonel of cavalry.

Approved April 2, 1862.

CHAP. XV.—*An Act to fix the compensation of the President of the Confederate States.* April 3, 1862.

The Congress of the Confederate States of America do enact, That Salary of the President fixed. Paya- the President shall receive for his services during his term of office, ble quarterly in adan annual salary of twenty-five thousand dollars, payable quarterly in vance. advance, to commence on the twenty-second day of February, eighteen hundred and sixty-two, the time at which he entered upon the duties of his office.

SEC. 2. *And be it further enacted,* That until a suitable Executive Rent of executive mansion shall be provided for the President, the rent of one suited to mansion to be paid the purpose shall be paid by the Government. by the Government.

Approved April 3, 1862.

CHAP. XVI.—*An Act making appropriations for the support of the Government from April first* April 3, 1862.
to the thirtieth of November, eighteen hundred and sixty-two, and for objects hereinafter expressed.

The Congress of the Confederate States of America do enact, That Aprropriations for the support of the the following sums be, and the same are hereby, appropriated out of Government from any money in the Treasury not otherwise appropriated, for the support April 1 to November 30, 1862. of the Government from April first to November thirtieth, eighteen hundred and sixty-two, and for the objects hereafter expressed:

Legislative.—For pay and mileage of Senators, seventy thousand Legislative. dollars.

For compensation of officers, clerks, &c., of the Senate, eight thousand four hundred and sixty-seven dollars.

For contingent expenses of the Senate, eight thousand dollars.

For pay and mileage of Members and Delegates of the House of Representatives, three hundred thousand dollars.

For compensation of officers, clerks, &c., of the House of Representatives, seven thousand one hundred dollars.

For contingent expenses of the House of Representatives, ten thousand dollars. .

For printing for Congress, fifteen thousand four hundred and sixteen dollars and sixty-seven cents.

Executive. *Executive.*—For compensation of the President of the Confederate States, seventeen thousand dollars.

For compensation of the Vice-President of the Confederate States, four thousand dollars.

For compensation of Private Secretary and Messenger of the President, one thousand three hundred dollars.

For contingent and telegraphic expenses of the Executive Office, one thousand five hundred dollars.

Office of Secretary of State; For compensation of the Secretary of State, Assistant Secretary of State, Clerks and Messenger, eight thousand two hundred and sixty-two dollars and sixty-seven cents.

of Secretary of Treasury; For compensation of the Secretary of the Treasury, Assistant Secretary of the Treasury, Auditors, Comptroller, Register and Treasurer, and clerks, and messengers and laborers in the Treasury Department, one hundred and twenty thousand dollars.

For incidental and contingent expenses of the Treasury Department, twenty-five thousand dollars.

of Secretary of War; For compensation of the Secretary of War, Assistant Secretary of War, Chiefs of Bureaus, and clerks and messengers in the War Department, eighty thousand dollars.

For Commissioner of Indian Affairs, clerks and messengers, and contingent expenses, four thousand dollars.

of Secretary of Navy; For compensation of the Secretary of the Navy, and clerks and messengers, &c., fourteen thousand six hundred and four dollars and forty-nine cents.

For incidental and contingent expenses of the Navy Department, eight thousand dollars.

of Postmaster General; For compensation of the Postmaster General, Chiefs of Bureaus, and clerks, messengers and laborers in the Post-Office Department, fifty thousand two hundred and thirty-two dollars and eighteen cents.

For temporary clerks in the Post-Office Department, eight thousand nine hundred and thirty-four dollars and seventeen cents.

For incidental and contingent expenses of the Post-Office Department, eight thousand three hundred and thirty four dollars and seventeen cents.

of Attorney General. For compensation of the Attorney General, Assistant Attorney General, clerks and messengers, eight thousand two hundred and sixty-six dollars and sixty-seven cents.

Superintendent Public Printing. For compensation of the Superintendent of Public Printing, and clerks and messengers in his office, two thousand eight hundred and sixty-six dollars and sixty-seven cents.

For incidental and contingent expenses of the Department of Justice, one thousand one hundred and sixty-six dollars and sixty-seven cents.

Printing. For printing for the several Executive Departments of the Government, one hundred and twenty-four thousand six hundred and eighty-four dollars and thirty-eight cents.

For rent of Executive Buildings and other expenses attending removal of seat of Government to Richmond, seven thousand dollars.

Judicial.—For salaries of Judges, Attorneys and Marshals, and for incidental and contingent expenses of Courts, one hundred and seventeen thousand dollars.

Miscellaneous.—To supply deficiencies in the revenue of the Post-Office Department, one million four hundred and fifty-one thousand six hundred and two dollars and thirty-one cents.

For engraving and printing Treasury notes, bonds and certificates of stock, and for paper for same, one hundred and twenty thousand dollars.

For compensation of agents, cost of materials and constructing, repairing and operating telegraph lines, &c., (act approved May 21, 1861,) thirty thousand dollars.

For salaries of Chief Collectors and Sub-Collectors of the War Tax, two hundred and fifty thousand dollars.

For wages of Assessors of War Tax, and for printing, three hundred thousand dollars.

For salaries of Commissioners under the Sequestration Act, and for clerk hire, and incidental and contingent expenses, seven thousand four hundred and twenty-one dollars and eighteen cents.

For preserving unfinished work upon the Charleston Custom-House, one thousand dollars.

For rent of the Executive Buildings, eleven thousand six hundred and twenty dollars.

Foreign Intercourse.—For salaries of Ministers, Commissioners, Secretaries, or other officers employed by the Government in relation to intercourse with foreign governments, and incidental, miscellaneous and contingent necessities, &c., sixty thousand dollars.

Public Debt.—For interest on the Public Debt, one million five hundred thousand dollars.

War Department.—For the pay of officers and privates of the army, volunteers and militia, in the public service of the Confederate States; and for Quartermasters supplies of all kinds, transportation and other necessary expenses, one hundred and fifty-five million dollars.

For the purchase of Subsistence Stores and Commissary property, twenty-nine million dollars.

For the Ordnance Service in all its branches, eleven million dollars.

For the Engineer Service, one million eight hundred thousand dollars.

For the Surgical and Medical Supplies of the Army, two million four hundred thousand dollars.

For contingent expenses of the Adjutant and Inspector General's Department, including office furniture, stationery, blanks, record books, &c., ten thousand dollars.

For incidental and contingent expenses of the Army, and of the Department of War, two hundred thousand dollars.

For floating defences of the Western Waters, five hundred thousand dollars, in accordance with the letter of the President of March 24, 1862, to be expended by the Secretary of War.

Indian Treaties.—To carry into effect treaty with the Creeks, of July 10, 1861, forty-nine thousand one hundred and forty dollars.

To carry into effect treaty with the Choctows and Chickasaws of July 12, 1861, sixty-one thousand one hundred and twenty-six dollars and eighty-nine cents.

To carry into effect treaty with the Cherokees, of October 7, 1861, four hundred and forty-six dollars and eighty-four cents.

Rent and removal of seat of Government

Judicial.

Miscellaneous.

Treasury notes, bonds, &c.

Telegraph lines.

Collectors of War Tax.

Assessors.

Commissioners, &c., under Sequestration Act.

Charleston Custom House.

Executive Buildings.

Foreign Intercourse.

Public Debt.

War Department.

Pay of officers, &c.

Subsistence Stores.

Ordnance Service.

Engineer Service.

Surgical and Medical Supplies.

Contingent expenses of Adjutant and Inspector General's Department.

Incidental and contingent expenses.

Floating defences.

Indian Treaties.

Choctaws and Chickasaws.

Cherokees.

Comanches.

To carry into effect treaty with the Comanches, of August 12th, 1861, one hundred and forty thousand, one hundred and sixty-seven dollars.

Osages.

To carry into effect treaty with the Osages, of October 2, 1861, two thousand and eighty-six dollars and fifty-eight cents.

Quapaws.

To carry into effect treaty with the Quapaws, of October 4, 1861, one thousand seven hundred and twenty-three dollars and twenty-three cents.

Reserve Indians.

To carry into effect treaty with the Reserve Indians, of August 12, 1861, one hundred and thirteen thousand one hundred and fifty-nine dollars.

Senecas and Shawnees.

To carry into effect treaty with the Senecas and Shawnees of October 4, 1861, three thousand six hundred and eleven dollars and sixty cents.

Superintendents and Agents, &c.

For pay of Superintendents and Agents, and incidental and contingent expenses of the several Indian agencies, eighteen thousand, two hundred and sixty-four dollars and twenty-eight cents.

Navy Department·Pay.

Navy Department.—For pay of the Navy, one million, seven hundred and sixteen thousand, two hundred and thirty-three dollars and twenty-nine cents.

Provisions and clothing.

For provisions and clothing, and contingencies in the Paymaster's Department, one million and four thousand eight hundred and fifty dollars.

Ordnance and Ordnance Stores.

For Ordnance and Ordnance Stores, one million, six hundred and sixty thousand dollars.

Nautical instruments.

For purchase of nautical instruments, books and charts, fifty thousand dollars.

Iron-clad vessels.

For construction of iron-clad vessels, three millions of dollars.

Equipments, &c., of vessels.

For equipment and repair of vessels, three hundred and fifty thousand dollars.

Fuel.

For purchase of fuel for steamers, navy-yards, and stations, one million dollars.

Medical supplies, &c.

For medical supplies and surgeon's necessaries, sixty-one thousand five hundred dollars.

Contingents.

For contingents enumerated, four hundred thousand dollars.

Hemp.

For purchase of hemp for the Navy, seventy-five thousand dollars.

Marine Corps.

For support of the Marine Corps (including Bounty) two hundred and forty-three thousand three hundred and twenty-two dollars.

Iron-clad vessels in Europe.

For construction of iron-clad vessels in Europe, two millions of dollars.

Territorial.

Territorial.—For salaries of the Governor and Commissioner of Indian Affairs and Secretary, Judges, Attorney and Marshal of Arizona Territory, six thousand five hundred and sixty dollars.

Arizona Territory.

For compensation of members of the Legislative Assembly of Arizona Territory and pay of officers, twelve thousand dollars.

For contingent expenses of the Legislative Assembly of Arizona Territory, including printing the laws, five thousand dollars.

For contingent expenses of Arizona Territory, seven hundred and seven dollars.

Approved April 3, 1862.

April 3, 1861.

Chap. XVII.—*An Act to amend An Act approved May,*10th, 1861, *entitled* "*An Act to amend An Act to provide for the public defence,*" *approved March 6th,* 1861.

The Congress of the Confederate States of America do enact, That the act approved May 10th, 1861, entitled an act to amend an act to provide for the public defence, approved March 6th, 1861, be, and the same is hereby so amended as to apply also to companies received into service for duty as Heavy Artillery.

Act of 1861, May 10, amended so as to apply to companies received as Heavy Artillery.

SEC. 2. The provisions of this act and of the act of May 10th, 1861, shall extend to all companies of Light and Heavy Artillery, which are now in, or may be hereafter received into the service, and all acts or parts of acts in conflict therewith are hereby repealed.

To extend to companies of Light and Heavy Artillery.

APPROVED April 3, 1862.

CHAP. XVIII.—*An Act to remit the duty on Railroad iron sufficient to complete the Alabama and Mississippi Rivers Railroad.*

April 7, 1862.

The Congress of the Confederate States of America do enact, That the duty on Railroad iron sufficient to complete the road on the route from Selma in Alabama to Meridian in Mississippi, held in bond, or which may hereafter be imported, and procured for the purpose stated be, and the same is hereby remitted : *Provided,* such iron shall be imported or purchased and used solely for the purpose stated, within three months from the date of the passage of this act.

Duty on certain railroad iron, remitted.

Proviso.

APPROVED April 7, 1862.

CHAP. XIX.—*An Act to provide for the organization of the Arkansas and Red River Superintendency of Indian Affairs, to regulate trade and intercourse with the Indians therein, and to preserve peace on the frontiers.*

April 8, 1862.

The Congress of the Confederate States of America do enact, That the Superintendency of Indian Affairs, for all the Indian country annexed to the Confederate States, that lies west of Arkansas and Missouri, north of Texas, and east of Texas and New Mexico, is hereby continued, and shall be called the Arkansas and Red River Superintendency of Indian Affairs, and the Superintendent thereof shall reside at Fort Smith, or Van Buren, in the State of Arkansas, until otherwise ordered by the President; shall give bond to the Confederate States, with sufficient sureties, in the sum of fifty thousand dollars, conditioned like those of the agents hereinafter prescribed, and shall receive a salary of two thousand five hundred dollars per annum, and be allowed a clerk, at an annual compensation of one thousand dollars.

Arkansas and Red River Superintendency of Indian Affairs.

Bond.

Condition.

SEC. 2. *And be it further enacted,* That the Superintendent of Indian Affairs for the Arkansas and Red River Superintendency, shall, within his superintendency, exercise a general supervision and control over the official conduct and accounts of all officers and persons employed by the Government in the Indian Department, under such regulations as shall be adopted or established by the President of the Confederate States; and may suspend such officers and persons from their offices or employments, for reasons forthwith to be communicated to the Secretary of War.

Duties.

May suspend officers and others.

SEC. 3. *And be it further enacted,* That the following Indian Agents shall be continued or appointed by the President, each of whom shall give bond, with two or more sureties, to the Confederate States, in the penal sum of twenty thousand dollars, if he disburses annually more than fifty thousand dollars ; and in ten thousand dollars, if he disburses annually less than fifty thousand dollars and more than twenty thousand

Indian Agents.

Bond.

Condition.

dollars; and in the sum of five thousand dollars, if he disburses annually less than twenty thousand dollars; conditioned for the faithful performance of the duties of their office, and that he will faithfully disburse, pay out and apply all moneys placed in his hands as agent, and render true and just accounts, as provided by the regulations of the War Department, of the receipt and expenditure of all moneys and property of every description entrusted to him, or coming to his hands in his official capacity, and pay over all balances and deliver all property that may, at any time, remain in his hands, on the order or re-

Compensation.

quisition of the War Department or Bureau of Indian Affairs; and each of such agents shall receive an annual compensation of fifteen hundred dollars; that is to say:

Osage Agency.

An Agent for the Osages, Senecas, Senecas and Shawnees and Quapaws, whose agency shall be known as the Osage Agency;

Cherokee Agency.

An Agent for the Cherokees, whose agency shall be known as the Cherokee Agency;

Creek Agency.

An Agent for the Creeks, whose agency shall be known as the Creek Agency;

Seminole Agency.

An agent for the Seminoles, whose agency shall be known as the Seminole Agency;

Choctaw and Chickasaw Agency.

An agent for the Choctaws and Chickasaws, whose agency shall be known as the Choctaw and Chickasaw Agency;

Wichita Reserve Agency.

An agent for the Wichitas, Comanches, Kichais, Huecos, Cado-ha-da-chos, Ta-hua-ca-ros, Ton-ca-wes, An-a dagh-cos, Ai-o-nais, Kickapoos, Shawnees and Delawares, in the country leased from the Choctaws and Chickasaws, whose agency shall be known as the Wichita Reserve Agency.

Discontinuance or transfer of agency.

SEC. 4. *And be it further enacted*, That the President shall be, and he is hereby, authorized, whenever he may deem it expedient, to discontinue any Indian Agency, or to transfer the same from the place or Nation designated by law, to such other place or Nation, as the public service may require.

Where agent to reside.

SEC. 5. *And be it further enacted*, That every Indian Agent shall reside and keep his agency upon the reserve selected for an agency, within the country of the Nation, or one of the Nations for which he may be agent, and shall not depart from the limits of such country at any time, or for any length of time, without the permission of the Superintendent, or of the Commissioner of Indian Affairs, granted for special and urgent reasons only, on penalty of immediate removal from office.

Limits of each agency.

SEC. 6. *And be it further enacted*, That the limits of each agency shall be the country of the Nation, or Nations, for which it is established.

Duties of agents.

And it shall be the duty of each agent, within the limits of his agency, to manage and superintend the intercourse with the Indians, agreeably to law; to obey all legal instructions given to him by the Secretary of War, the Commissioner of Indian Affairs, or the Superintendent of Indian Affairs, and to carry into effect such regulations as may be prescribed by the President.

Additional security

SEC. 7. *And be it further enacted*, That the President may at any time require additional security, and, in larger amounts, from all persons charged or entrusted, under the laws of the Confederate States, with the transportation, disbursement or application of money, goods or effects of any kind, on account of the Indian Department.

Interpreter allowed each agency.

SEC. 8. *And be it further enacted*, That one interpreter shall be allowed to each agency, except that for the Wichitas and other bands,

Compensation.

who shall receive an annual compensation of four hundred dollars; and that for the Wichita Agency one may be allowed for each different language spoken, each of whom shall receive a compensation of four hundred dollars per annum; except those for the Comanches, and for the Wichitas, Hue-cos, and Ta-hua-ca-ros, each of whom shall receive a compensation of four hundred dollars per annum, or, in lieu of part of these, one interpreter may be employed for the Comanches, Wichitas, Hue-cos, Ta-hua-ca-ros, Cado-ho-da-chos, and An-a-dagh-cos, at a compensation of one thousand dollars per annum. These interpreters shall be selected by the Superintendent, on the recommendation of the respective agents, or upon his own knowledge of their competency and good character, and may be suspended by the agent, from pay and duty, the circumstances being by him reported to the Superintendent for final action. In the appointment of interpreters, preference shall be given to persons of Indian descent, and of the same nation, for which they are appointed, if such can be found, who are properly qualified for the execution of their duties. Preference given to persons of Indian descent.

Sec. 9. *And be it further enacted*, That blacksmiths and wagon-makers shall, in like manner, be employed, wherever required by Treaty stipulations, and shall receive such compensation as may be fixed by treaties, or in the absence of such provision by treaty, an annual compensation of not more than seven hundred and fifty dollars; and if they furnish their shop and tools, an additional compensation of one hundred and twenty dollars per annum: and their assistants shall be allowed an annual compensation of two hundred and forty dollars; and whenever other mechanics, teachers or physicians are required by Treaty stipulations to be provided, they shall be, in like manner employed, and the male teachers shall receive an annual compensation of not more than one thousand dollars, female teachers an annual compensation of not more than six hundred dollars; physicians an annual compensation of not more than one thousand dollars, and mechanics an annual compensation of not more than seven hundred and fifty dollars. Farmers and laborers, required by Treaty stipulations to be furnished, shall be employed by the Agents, subject to the approval of the Superintendent, unless the Superintendent himself sees fit to employ them, which he may do; and their compensation shall not, in any case, be greater for farmers than six hundred dollars per annum, and for laborers, than forty dollars per month. Blacksmiths and wagon-makers.
Compensation.
Their assistants.
Other mechanics, teachers or physicians.
Compensation.

Sec. 10. *And be it further enacted*, That the salaries and annual compensations provided by this act shall be in full of all emoluments or allowances whatever, except such fees as are hereinafter specially allowed to be received: *Provided, however*, That reasonable allowances and provisions may be made for office rent and office contingencies; and that when the Superintendent or Agent is required, in the performance of the duties prescribed by this act, to travel from one place to another, he shall be allowed the same expenses of travel, or mileage and transportation, as may be allowed to officers of the army, and such additional allowance for transportation and expenses of traveling in the Indian country, as the Secretary may be satisfied is just; but *provided, also*, that no allowance shall be made to any such officer for travel or expenses, in going to the Seat of Government to settle his accounts, or returning therefrom, unless ordered thither for that purpose, by the Commissioner of Indian Affairs, or Secretary of War. Salaries, &c., to be in full of all emoluments, except fees.
Proviso.
Proviso.

Sec. 11. *And be it further enacted*, That no person shall hold more than one office under this act at one and the same time; nor shall any Agent or Interpreter receive any salary or compensation, while absent from the Agency, without leave of the Superintendent or Commissioner of Indian Affairs; and if an Interpreter be absent, without leave of No person to hold more than one office.
Agent or Interpreter absent without leave, to receive no pay;

and Interpreter may be removed from office.

the Superintendent or Commissioner, for more than sixty days, at any one time, it shall be sufficient cause of his removal from office.

Superintendents, agents or interpreters, not to trade with Indians;

Sec. 12. *And be it further enacted*, That no Superintendent, Agent or Interpreter, shall have any interest or concern in any mercantile establishment in the Indian country, or in any trade carried on with the Indians, under the penalty of immediate removal from office, and perpetual disqualification to hold any office under the Indian Bureau;

nor be concerned in any claims on behalf of the Indians;

and neither of them shall be concerned or interested in any claim on behalf of the Indians against the Confederate States, of any kind

nor to receive any compensation for certain services.

whatever, nor receive any compensation fee or gratuity whatever from the Indians, in any shape, manner or form, for any services in the presentation or recovery of any such claim, or the collection of any moneys from the Government, for individual Indians, or for the Na-

Penalty.

tion; and any person so offending shall be deemed guilty of misdemeanor in office, corruption and extortion, shall be forthwith removed, and, upon conviction thereof by indictment, shall be punished by fine of not less than five hundred, nor more than five thousand dollars, and imprisonment not less than six months nor more than five years, and be condemned to make restitution of the whole amount of the compensation, fee or gratuity, so received, with interest at the rate of ten per cent. per annum from the time when he received the same; and shall also be forever disqualified to hold any office, civil or military, under the Confederate States.

Payments of annuities.

Sec. 13. *And be it further enacted*, That payment of all annuities, and other sums of money, stipulated by treaty or directed by law, to be paid to the Cherokees, Creeks, Choctaws and Chickasaws, shall be made to the Treasurer of each Nation, or to such other person or persons, as the legislative power of each may direct; and the moneys so received shall be disposed of by the authorities of the Nation, without any interference on the part of any Department, Bureau or office of the Government of the Confederate States. Payments of all sums of money to be made to the Seminole Nation, and to any other tribes or bands of Indians in the said superintendency, shall be made to the Treasurer, Chiefs, or *per capita*, as the treaties may provide, or, in the absence of treaty provisions, as the Commissioner of Indian Affairs shall, in each case, direct.

By whom payments of moneys to be made.

Sec. 14. *And be it further enacted*, That all payments of moneys to any of said nations, tribes or bands, shall be made by such persons as the President shall designate for that purpose; and that he may, at his discretion, entrust military officers with such payments; in which case the duty shall be performed by them, without other compensation than the ordinary allowances for travel and transportation.

Penalty against Agent for embezzlement;

Sec. 15. *And be it further enacted*, That if any Agent of the Confederate States for any nation, tribe or band of Indians, shall convert to his own use, or improperly withhold from any of the Indians under his charge, any article, or any part or quantity of any article of provisions, clothing, merchandize, or other thing whatever, placed in his hands by the Government of the Confederate States, for distribution or delivery to such Indians, or any moneys, to any amount whatever, placed in his hands to be paid to them, or to be expended for their benefit, whether by the United States heretofore, or by the Confede-

or for employing person employed by the government to assist the Indians;

rate States heretofore or hereafter, or shall employ in his own private service and affairs any person employed by the Government to labor for or assist the Indians, or shall receive from any contractor any share

or for receiving from contractor any share of profits.

of profits, per centage, compensation, or gratuity whatever, every such agent, so offending, shall be deemed guilty of felony, and on conviction thereof in the proper court, shall be fined not less than five hundred, nor more than fifty thousand dollars, sentenced to make full restitution to the Confederate States, and be imprisoned, at hard labor, not less than two, nor more than ten years.

Sec. 16. *And be it further enacted*, That no exchange of funds shall be made by any superintendent or agent, or, by any other disbursing officer or agent of the Government, of any grade or denomination, whatsoever, employed in, or connected with the Indian service, other than an exchange for gold and silver, or Treasury notes; and every such disbursing officer, when the means for his disbursements are furnished him in gold and silver, shall make his payments in the identical moneys so furnished, or when those means are furnished to him in Treasury warrants or drafts, shall either cause such warrants or drafts to be presented at their place of payment, and properly paid, according to law, and shall make his payments in the identical moneys so received for the drafts furnished; unless, in either case, he can exchange the means in his hands, for the gold and silver, or other kind of funds, in which they are payable. at or for more than par; and any officer, in any way, violating the provisions of this section, shall be forthwith removed from office, and upon conviction thereof, upon indictment in the proper District Court, shall be punished by fine of not less than one thousand, nor more than ten thousand dollars, be imprisoned, not less than six months, nor more than two years, and be, thereafter incapable of holding any office of trust or profit, under the Confederate States.

No exchange of funds allowed except for gold and silver, or Treasury notes.

Payments to be made in the identical moneys or funds received.

Penalty for failure.

Sec. 17. *And be it further enacted*, That no superintendent, agent, or other officer mentioned in the sixteenth section of this act, shall either directly or *or* indirectly sell or dispose of, to any person or persons, firm or corporation whatsoever, any Treasury note, draft, warrant, or other public security in his hands, as such officer, and not his private property, at par, where he can obtain a premium on the same, or for any less than the current premium, at the time and place; nor shall sell or dispose of any specie funds, with or without a premium, for any other funds; nor shall loan any of the funds in his hands to any person whatever, nor sell the same; or any draft, warrant, or other security, to any person whatever, upon time, or to receive the proceeds at a future day, however near; and if any such officer shall, in any way, violate the preceding provisions of this section, or shall receive, directly or indirectly, any premium whatever, upon the sale or disposition, or exchange, of any funds, specie, warrant, draft or security, by way of exchange, or otherwise, and shall not make true return of such premium so received, and account for the same, by charging it in his accounts to the credit of the Confederate States, he shall be forthwith dismissed from office; and shall, in addition, upon conviction upon indictment in the proper district court, be punished and become incapable, in the same manner as is provided in the sixteenth section of this act : *Provided*, That nothing in this act shall be so construed as to allow disbursing officers to make payment in any other funds than specie or Treasury notes.

Penalty against officers for selling or disposing of Treasury notes, drafts, warrants, etc.

To account for premium received.

Proviso.

Sec. 18. *And be it further enacted*, That the President shall be, and he is hereby, authorised to cause such rations as he shall judge proper, and as can be spared from the army provisions, without injury to the service, to be issued under such regulations as he shall see fit to establish; or beef and flour, in lieu thereof, to be purchased and issued by the officers commanding military posts, to Indians who may visit such posts, and by agents to those who may visit their agencies, and to councils called by authority of the Confederate States; and special accounts of these issues shall be kept and rendered, and the

Rations allowed Indians.

Special accounts thereof to be kept.

Secretary of War may authorise the agents for the Creeks, Seminoles, Osages and Reserve Indians to expend a sum not larger than three hundred dollars per annum, in furnishing provisions to Indians attend-

Proviso. ing councils and payments of annuities : *Provided,* That no money shall be expended for this purpose which has not been previously appropriated by law.

Accounts of disbursements to be settled annually. Sec. 19. *And be it further enacted,* That all persons whatsoever, charged or entrusted with the disbursement or application of money, goods or effects of any kind, for the benefit of the Indians, shall settle their accounts annually at the War Department, on the first day of

Copies of same to be laid before Congress. October ; and copies of same shall be laid annually before Congress, at the commencement of the ensuing session, by the proper accounting officers, together with the list of the names of all persons to whom money, goods or effects had been delivered within the year, for the benefit of Indians, specifying the amount of each, and the object for which each sum or quantity was intended, and showing who are delinquents, if any, in forwarding their accounts, according to the provisions of this act ; and also a list of the names of all persons appointed or employed under this act, with the date of appointment or employment of each, and the salary or pay of each.

Who not permitted to trade with Indians without license. Sec. 20. *And be it further enacted,* That no person, other than a member of the particular tribe or nation under treaty stipulations, or a member of another Indian nation or tribe, permitted to trade by the authorities of the nation or tribe. within whose limits he so trades, shall be permitted to trade with the Indians, in the Indian country aforesaid, without a license therefor from the agent for the nation or tribes in whose country the trade is to be carried on ; and which li-

By whom license to be issued. cense, in the Cherokee, Creek, Seminole, Choctaw and Chickasaw countries, must be granted by and with the advice and consent of the Legislature or General Council of such nation : *Provided,* That no li-

Proviso. cense shall be necessary to authorise the selling from wagons, or otherwise, flour, bacon, fruits, and other provisions, brought from the Confederate States, or wagons, agricultural implements, domestic animals or arms brought from any of the same. Each license shall be

Term of license. issued for a term not exceeding three years ; and all licenses granted

Renewal of license. before the passage of this act may be renewed by the agents, in their discretion, without the advice or consent of the legislature or council, to continue until the expiration of the year one thousand eight hundred and sixty-two.

Person obtaining license to give bond. Sec. 21. *And be it further enacted,* That the person or persons obtaining a license. must give bond in a penal sum not exceeding five

Condition of bond. thousand dollars, with one or more sureties, approved and certified to be sufficient, by the agent to whom the application is made, conditioned that such person or persons will faithfully observe and obey all laws and regulations for the government of trade and intercourse with the Indian tribes, adopted or enacted by the Confederate States, or any department thereof, and will, in no respect, violate the same. And the

When license may be revoked. Superintendent of Indian Affairs shall have power to revoke and cancel any license whenever he shall be satisfied that the person licensed has violated any of the said laws or regulations, or that, for any other good reason, it would be improper to permit him to remain in the Indian country.

Trading without license. Sec. 22. *And be it further enacted,* That any person, other than a member of the nation or tribe, under treaty stipulations, or a member of another Indian nation or tribe, permitted to trade by the authorities of the nation or tribe within whose limits he so trades, who shall attempt to reside in any part of the Indian country as a trader, or to introduce goods, or to trade therein, without a license duly obtained. shall forfeit all merchandise offered for sale to the Indians, or found in his possession, and shall, moreover, forfeit and pay the sum of five hundred dollars, to be recovered by action of debt, in the name of the Confederate States, or adjudged on conviction and forfeiture of the goods, one-half thereof to be paid to the informer, and the other half to the nation or tribe in whose country the offence is committed, to which nation or tribe also all the goods forfeited, and all wines and liquors confiscated, shall be given and belong.

Forfeiture.

SEC. 23. *And be it further enacted,* That no license to trade with Indians shall be granted to any person or persons other than a citizen or citizens of the Confederate States.

Licenses to be granted only to citizens of the C S.

SEC. 24. *And be it further enacted,* That any agent may refuse an application for a license to trade, if he is satisfied that the applicant is a person of bad character, or that it would be improper to permit him to remain in the Indian country; or if a license previously granted to him has been revoked, or a forfeiture decreed of any bond previously given by him: *Provided,* That any person, whose application is thus denied, may appeal to the Superintendent of Indian Affairs, whose decision shall be final.

When agent may refuse application for license.

Proviso.

SEC. 25. *And be it further enacted,* That if any licensed trader shall purchase of an Indian any gun, or any instrument of husbandry, or blanket, cooking utensil, or other article, furnished the Indians by the Confederate States, his license shall be immediately revoked, and he shall forfeit and pay, for the use of such Indians, to the Confederate States, the sum of fifty dollars for every article so purchased.

Penalty against licensed trader for purchasing certain articles furnished the Indians.

SEC. 26. *And be it further enacted,* That no person, not being a member of the nation or tribe, or otherwise authorised by law or treaty, shall drive or otherwise convey, or cause, or permit to be otherwise conveyed, any horses, mules, or cattle, to range and graze in any part of the Indian country, without the consent of the authorities of the nation or tribe previously obtained, under the penalty of one dollar a head for each animal so pastured, which may be collected by the authorities of the nation, and payment enforced, if necessary, by the seizure of the cattle: *Provided,* That movers, and other persons driving stock through the country, may halt from place to place, for such reasonable length of time as will be sufficient to recruit their stock, but no longer, doing the same in good faith.

Ranging and grazing in Indian country

Penalty against.

Proviso.

SEC. 27. *And be it further enacted,* That the Superintendent of Indian Affairs, and each agent within his agency, shall have authority, and it shall be the duty of each, to remove from the Indian country all persons found therein contrary to law or treaty; and all other persons, not Indians, and not by birth and blood members of the particular nation, whose presence is, in his opinion, dangerous or mischievous; and shall have power to call upon the officer commanding any military post to aid him in so doing, and enforce his orders in that behalf: *Provided,* That the person so removed by an agent may appeal to the Superintendent, whose decision thereon shall be final.

Removal of intruders.

Proviso.

SEC. 28. *And be it further enacted,* That the provisions of law invalidating any purchase of lands from an Indian nation or tribe, shall no longer be in force, in respect to the Cherokee, Creek, Seminole, Choctaw and Chickasaw Nations, each of which may, under special or general laws passed for that purpose, sell parcels of their lands, or convey parcels of the same by legislative grants, in fee simple, to individual purchasers or grantees; and such sales or grants shall be valid in law and equity, in the absence of fraud, and shall only be impeached in the same manner, as if they had been made by a State.

Sale of lands by certain Indian nations, made valid.

2

Penalty for attempting to cause infraction of Indian treaties, etc.

Sec. 29. *And be it further enacted,* That if any person shall send, make, carry or deliver any talk, speech, message or letter, to any Indian nation, tribe, band, chief or individual, with intent to produce a contravention, or infraction of any treaty, or other law of the Confederate States, or to disturb the peace and tranquillity of the Confederate States, or to make such nation, tribe, band, chief or Indian dissatisfied with their relations with the Confederate States, or uneasy, or discontented, the person so offending shall, on conviction thereof, be punished by fine not exceeding ten thousand dollars, nor less than two thousand dollars, and by imprisonment not less than two, nor more than ten years ; and the intent above mentioned shall be conclusively inferred from the fact of knowledge of the contents of any such talk, speech, message, or letter in writing.

For correspondence with foreign powers, with such intent.

Sec. 30. *And be it further enacted,* That if any person, whether an Indian or a white person, shall carry on a correspondence, by letter or otherwise, with any foreign nation or power, or with any department or office of such foreign nation or power, with intent to induce such nation or power, department or office. to give assistance or encouragement to any Indian nation, tribe, chief or chiefs, individual or individuals, in waging war, or commencing, or continuing hostilities against the Confederate States, or in the violation of any existing treaty, or shall attempt to alienate the confidence of any Indian or Indians, from the Government of the Confederate States, he shall be punished, if the offence be committed in time of peace, as in the last preceding section is provided ; and, if the offence be committed in time of war, with such foreign nation or power, the punishment thereof shall be death, to be inflicted as in other cases of capital offences.

For carrying on correspondence with any power with which the C. S. is at war.

Sec. 31. *And be it further enacted,* That any Indian of any Nation or Tribe, between which and the Confederate States a Treaty of friendship and alliance has been concluded, who shall while the Confederate States are at war with any other States, Nation or power, carry on any correspondence with such States, Nation or power, or any Department or office thereof, or shall attend any Council, or hold any talk or conference, in the Indian country or elsewhere, with any officer of such States, Nation or power, shall, on conviction thereof, be punished with death, to be inflicted as in other cases of capital punishment.

Emissaries from such powers, how punished.

Sec. 32. *And be it further enacted,* That any emissary from any State or States, nation or power, with which the Confederate States may be at war, found in the Indian Country, and any Indian therein apprehended, returning from any council, talk or conferences with any officer of the enemy, or after such return, shall be considered a spy, and punished by death by hanging, to be inflicted upon the sentence of a Military Court, to be ordered by the General commanding in such Indian country.

Twice the value of property stolen or injured to be paid to friendly Nations.

Sec. 33. *And be it further enacted,* That whenever the property of any member of a friendly Nation, or Tribe of Indians, is unlawfully stolen, taken, converted, destroyed or injured, by any white person, not a member by birth, adoption, or otherwise, of said Nation or Tribe, or by a member of any other friendly Indian Nation or Tribe, within the Indian country, if conviction be had of the person offending, for the crime, misdemeanor or trespass so committed, or recovery of damage therefor in a civil suit, the person so offending shall be sentenced or adjudged to pay the person injured a sum equal to twice the just value of the property so stolen, taken, converted or destroyed, or twice the amount of damages sustained by the injury of the same. And if the same cannot be recovered of the party, or if, for any cause, conviction or recovery cannot be had then, upon the said offence, and the value of the property or the full amount of damage being established, upon investigation by the Agent of the Confederate States, for the Nation or Tribe, to which the person injured belongs, the full value of the property, or the full amount of damage sustained, with any other actual damage caused thereby, and interest and expenses, or so much thereof as cannot be collected of the party, shall be paid out of the Treasury of the Confederate States: *Provided*, That no person shall be entitled to such payment out of the Treasury, if he, or any of the Nation or Tribe, to which he belongs, shall have sought private revenge for the injury in question, or attempted to obtain satisfaction by violence or fraud.

Unless revenge be attempted.

Sec. 34. *And be it further enacted*, That if any member or members of any Indian Nation or Tribe, within the Indian country, shall unlawfully take, convert, destroy, or injure any property of any person lawfully within such country, or shall, in any one of the Confederate States, or in any Territory or Province of the Confederate States, or within the limits of any other Indian Nation or Tribe, steal, take, convert, destroy or injure any property belonging to any citizen or inhabitant of the Confederate States, or of any Territory or Province thereof, or of any member of any other friendly Nation or Tribe of Indians, other than that to which he or they belong, such citizen, inhabitant or member of a friendly Nation or Tribe, may, by himself, or by his attorney or agent, make complaint to the Agent of the Confederate States, for the Nation or Tribe to which the offender may belong, or to the Superintendent, who shall take and hear the proof of the truth of such complaint, and if satisfied of the truth thereof, and that the offender belongs to the Nation or Tribe alleged, shall demand prompt satisfaction from such Nation or Tribe; and if satisfaction be not made within the space of six months thereafter, by payment by the Nation or Tribe of the value of the property taken, stolen, converted or destroyed, and all actual damages and expenses sustained in consequence thereof, and interest on the said value from the time of taking or conversion, or of the amount of damage sustained by the injury done the property, with like actual damages, expenses and interest, then full report shall be made thereof to the Commissioner of Indian Affairs; and thereupon the amount so ascertained shall be directed to be deducted from any annuity or other moneys payable to said Nation or Tribe; or if there be none such, then the President shall take such other steps to enforce payment as may seem to him fit: and in the meantime, the amount shall be paid out of the Treasury of the Confederate States: *Provided*, That if such injured party, his representative, attorney or agent, shall, in any way, violate any of the provisions of this Act, by seeking revenge or redress by violence, or any other illegal means, he shall forfeit all his claim to indemnification; that any such claim, not presented to the Agent or Superintendent within three years, after the commission of the alleged injury, shall be forever barred; that nothing herein contained shall be construed to prevent the legal apprehension and punishment of any Indian, or member of any Nation or Tribe, that may so have offended; and that from the decision of the Agent, the complainant, or the Nation or Tribe may appeal to the Superintendent, and from his decision to the Commissioner of Indian Affairs, whose judgment shall be final in the premises: *Provided*, That the Indian country shall not be deemed to include the residence of Indian Tribes or persons within the limits of any of the Confederate States.

Persons to be indemnified for property destroyed by Indians.

If no revenge be sought.

Limitation.

How this act to be construed.

Appeal.

Proviso.

Sec. 35. *And be it further enacted*, That any proceeding instituted under the authority of the United States to obtain satisfaction in any

Proceedings under the authority of the U. S. to obtain satisfaction; how to be carried on. case mentioned in the two preceding sections, shall be carried on and completed before the authorities of the Confederate States, as if no change of government had taken place; and that if any final order or adjudication had been made in any such case, by the proper officer of the United States, before the assumption of jurisdiction by the Confederate States, on the twenty-first day of May, eighteen hundred and sixty-one, the same shall still be deemed and taken as final, and be carried out, as if made by the same officer of the Confederate States.

Punishment for forging or counterfeiting coin, or the securities of the Confederate States; Sec. 36. *And be it further enacted,* That so much and such parts of the laws of the Confederate States, as provide for punishing the counterfeiting the coin of the United States, or any other current coin, and the uttering such forged or counterfeit coin, or the counterfeiting or forging the securities of the Confederate States, and the uttering such

robbing the mail and other offences. forged or counterfeit securities, and the robbing of the mail, and for punishing the violations of the neutrality laws, and resistance to the process of the Confederate States, and all the provisions of the acts of the Provisional Congress, providing for the common defence and welfare, so far as the same are not legally inapplicable, shall hereafter be in force in the Indian country ; and offences against the same by any person whatever, shall be punished by indictment in the proper court of the Confederate States having jurisdiction.

Laws of the Confederate States punishing felonies, declared to be in force in the Indian country. Sec. 37. *And be it further enacted,* That so much of the laws of the Confederate States, as provide for the punishment of forgery or counterfeiting, perjury, subornation of perjury, rape, arson, shooting with intent to kill or maim, burglary, robbery, larceny, or any other crime amounting to felony at common law, or by statute, committed in any place whatever, within the sole and exclusive jurisdiction of the Con-

Proviso. federate States, shall be in force in the Indian country : *Provided,* That none of the same shall extend or apply to crimes committed by a member of any Tribe or Nation, by birth, adoption or otherwise, as hereinafter defined, or by any negro or mulatto, bond or free, against the person or property of a member of the same, or any other Nation or Tribe, by birth, adoption, or otherwise, as hereinafter defined, or of any negro or mulatto, bond or free ; but these offences shall be within the sole and exclusive jurisdiction of the Tribunals of the Nation or Tribe, within whose country they are committed ; excepting, however, such offences, when committed in the Choctaw and Chickasaw country, west of the ninety-eighth parallel of longitude, by an Indian of any one of the Bands settled therein, against the person or property of such a member of the Choctaw and Chickasaw Nation, or by such a member of one of these Nations against the person or property of an Indian of any one of these Bands, as to which offences so committed, the said laws shall be in force, and the offenders be tried therefor in the proper court of the Confederate States.

Penalty against gaming. Sec. 38. *And be it further enacted,* That, if any person, not being a negro or mulatto, or a member by birth, adoption, or otherwise, as hereinafter defined, of the Nation or Tribe in which the act is committed, shall, in the Indian country, open, exhibit and deal at, or be interested in, by furnishing means, or sharing the profits of the game, any game of faro, monte, or other banking game ; at which game betters bet against the game, bank or dealer, or shall set up, exhibit and permit to be bet against, at, or upon, or be interested, by furnishing means, or sharing the profits in any roulette table, or other table, or game of like nature, at which game or table, any person shall bet money, checks or counters, representing money or any other thing of value, or shall bet on credit, every such person shall be deemed guilty of an offence against the Confederate States, cognizable upon indictment or presentment by the District Court having jurisdiction over such Indian country, and upon conviction, shall be fined one thousand dollars, and imprisoned at hard labor not less than ninety days, nor more than two years; and it shall be the duty of the Agent, if he becomes cognizant of the carrying on of any such game or table, to arrest the parties and seize all the tables, boxes and other implements used, and all checks and moneys found thereon and therein; as also any civil officer of the proper Nation may do; all which articles and money, when seized, shall belong, one-half to the officer seizing the same, and one-half to the Nation wherein they are seized. And any officer of the Nation arresting such person shall deliver him to the Agent, who shall investigate the case, and commit, bail, or discharge, as in other cases; but no person so arrested and bailed shall be permitted to remain in the Nation, but shall forthwith be removed therefrom.

Duty of agents and officers.

Forfeiture.

SEC. 39. *And be it further enacted,* That if any person who has taken, or is concerned in any contract with the Confederate States, or with any agent or officer thereof, for furnishing provisions to any Indians whatever, shall be guilty of defrauding them by the issue of a less quantity than they, or any part or one of them, are or is entitled to, and receiving pay for the quantity which should have been issued, or of receiving pay in any otherwise, for issues not made, or provisions not issued, such person shall be deemed guilty of felony, and, on conviction thereof in the proper Court, shall be fined not less than five hundred, nor more than ten thousand dollars, sentenced to full restitution to the Confederate States, and be imprisoned at hard labor not less than two, nor more than twenty years.

Punishment of contractors for fraud.

SEC. 40. *And be it further enacted,* That if any person shall convey, transport or introduce, or attempt to convey, transport or introduce, by land or water carriage, into any Indian Nation or Tribe, for the purposes of sale, exchange, barter or traffic, or knowing that the same is intended to be sold, exchanged, bartered or trafficked, anywhere in the Indian country, any spirituous or intoxicating liquors or mixtures, or wines of any kind or description whatever, (unless the same are provided and to be used by some licensed trader, druggist, apothecary or physician, for purposes purely medicinal,) every person concerned in such offence shall forfeit and pay a fine of not less than five hundred, and not more than two thousand dollars, upon indictment or presentment before the proper court, to be paid, one-half to the informer, and the other half to the Nation or Tribe, into the country whereof such introduction was effected or attempted, and be imprisoned not less than three months, nor more than one year.

Penalty for selling liquors to Indians.

SEC. 41. *And be it further enacted,* That if the Superintendent of Indian Affairs, or the agent for any Nation or Tribe, or any Commanding officer of a military post, or any judge or commissioner of a court of the Confederate States is informed, or has reason to suspect, that any person whatever has introduced, or is about to introduce, any spirituous or intoxicating liquors or mixtures, or any wine, into any part of the Indian country, in violation of this Act, it shall be the duty of such superintendent, agent, officer, judge or commissioner, in accordance with such regulations as may be established by the President of the Confederate States, to cause the houses, stores, boats, wagons, carriages, packages and other places of deposit of such person to be searched; and if any such liquors, mixtures or wine are found, all the goods of such person of which they form a part, the boats on which they are found, the wagons, carriages and packages conveying or containing the same, to an amount not exceeding twenty times the value

Introducing liquors into the Indian Territory.

Duties of Superintendents, Agents, &c.

Searches and seizures.

of the said liquors, mixtures and wine, shall be seized and delivered
to the proper officer, and be proceeded against by libel in the proper
court, and forfeited to the use of the Nation or Tribe into which the
same is introduced, or attempted to be introduced; and if the person
offending is a licensed trader, his license shall be forthwith revoked,
and suit instituted on his bond. And it shall, moreover, be lawful for
any person in the civil or military service of the Confederate States, or
for any Indian, a member by birth, adoption or otherwise, of any Indian Nation or Tribe, to take and destroy any such liquors, mixtures or
wine found in the Indian country in violation of this Act.

Sec. 42. *And be it further enacted,* That if any licensed trader, or
any other person (other than a member by birth, adoption, or otherwise,
of any Indian Nation or Tribe) shall, within the limits of such Nation
or Tribe, sell, under the pretense of a gift, or otherwise, to any Indian,
or exchange or barter with any Indian, of either sex, and of full or
mixed blood, any intoxicating liquor or mixture, or any wine, in any
quantity, large or small, such person shall, on conviction thereof, upon
indictment, be punished by fine of not less than five hundred dollars,
and imprisoned not less than ten days nor more than six months, which
fine shall be paid, one-half to the informer and the other half to the
Nation or Tribe, as other fines.

Sec. 43. *And be it further enacted,* That when goods, liquors or
other articles whatever are seized for any violation of this Act, they
shall be proceeded against in the manner directed to be observed in
the case of goods, wines or merchandize brought into the Confederate
States in violation of the Revenue Laws.

Sec. 44. *And be it further enacted,* That if any person whatever
shall, within the limits of the Indian country, set up or continue any
distillery for manufacturing ardent spirits, he shall forfeit and pay a
penalty of one thousand dollars, on indictment, for such offence, and
the buildings so used, with the still and all other furniture and contents
shall be confiscated, one-half the penalty to the informer, and the other
half, with the buildings, still, furniture and contents to the Nation or
Tribe; and it shall be the duty of the Superintendent, or proper agent,
to seize and turn over the same to the Nation or Tribe.

Sec. 45. *And be it further enacted,* That for any penalty accruing
under this Act, the informer may sue and recover the same in an action of debt, *qui tam,* in the name of the Confederate States, before
any court having jurisdiction of the same in any State or District in
which the offender may be found to be served with process.

Sec. 46. *And be it further enacted,* That it shall be lawful for the
military force of the Confederate States, to be employed in such manner and under such regulations as the President may direct, and upon
the requisition of a Superintendent, or of an Agent, in the apprehension of any person offending against any provision of this Act, or found
in the Indian country, in violation of its provisions, or of any Treaty
stipulation, and him immediately to convey from such country, and dispose of, as directed by the proper officer, or authority, to be proceeded
against, if the case require it, in due course of law; and also in the
examination and seizure of stores, boats, wagons, carriages and packages, authorized by this Act, and in preventing the introduction of persons and property into the Indian country contrary to law; which persons and property shall be proceeded against according to law: *Provided,* That no person apprehended by military force as aforesaid, shall
be detained longer than five days after the arrest, and before removal.
And all officers and soldiers, who may have such person or persons, in
custody, shall treat them with all the humanity, which the circum-

Forfeiture.

Liquors may be dis-
trained.

Punishment for sell-
ing liquors under
fraudulent pretences.

Proceedings against
property seized.

Penalty for manu-
facturing liquors in
the Indian Country.

How to be recover-
ed.

Duties of the mili-
tary in enforcing this
Act.

Treatment of per-
son arrested.

stances will possibly permit ; and every officer and soldier, who shall be guilty of maltreating any such person, while in custody, shall suffer such punishment as a court martial shall direct.

SEC. 47. *And be it further enacted*, That every person shall be considered a member of the Cherokee, Creek, Seminole, Choctaw and Chickasaw Nations, for the purposes of this act, whose mother was a member of the same, or whose father was so, though married to a white woman, if both were domiciled in the nation when the party was born, and if such party still resides therein ; or who has with his or her consent, been adopted by the act of the legislature or general council of the nation, and therein continues to reside ; or who has married a member of the nation, and is settled and resides therein ; or who is permanently domiciled therein with the consent of the nation, and is permitted to vote at elections. *Who considered members of the Indian nations.*

SEC. 48. *And be it further enacted*, That the reservations or selections for military posts and forts in the Indian country, shall be within the sole and exclusive jurisdiction of the Confederate States, as also shall the reservations for agencies in the several nations and tribes ; and that all the laws of the Confederate States in force, in any other place within such sole and exclusive jurisdiction shall be in force within the limits of all such reservations and selections, and offences committed therein be punished accordingly : *Provided*, That as to all members of the nation, within whose limits any agency reservation is situated, who commit any offence therein against any law of such nation, upon the person or property of any other member of such nation, or against its police regulations, the laws of such nation shall govern, and they shall or may be punished thereunder, by the tribunals of the nation. *Exclusive jurisdiction of the C. S.* *Proviso.*

SEC. 49. *And be it further enacted*, That whenever any person, who is a member of any Indian nation or tribe, shall be indicted for any offence in any court of the Confederate States, he shall be entitled, as of common right, to subpoena, and if necessary, compulsory process for all such witnesses in his behalf, as his counsel may think necessary for his defence, and the cost of process for such witnesses, and of service thereof, and the fees and mileage of such witnesses shall be paid by the Confederate States, being afterwards made, if practicable, in case of conviction, of the property of the accused. And whenever the accused is not able to employ counsel, the court shall assign him one experienced counsel for his defence, who shall be paid by the Confederate States a reasonable compensation for his services, to be fixed by the court, and paid upon the certificate of the judge. *Rights secured to party indicted.* *When court may assign counsel.*

SEC. 50. *And be it further enacted*, That the provisions of all such acts of the Congress of the Confederate States, as may now be in force, or as may hereafter be enacted, for the purpose of carrying into effect the provisions of the Constitution, in regard to the redelivery or return of fugitive slaves, or fugitives from labor and service, shall extend to, and be in full force, within the said Indian country ; and shall also apply to all cases of escape of fugitive slaves from any Indian nation or tribe into any other Indian nation or tribe; or, into one of the Confederate States, the obligation upon each such nation, tribe or State to redeliver such slaves, being, in every case, as complete as if they had escaped from another State, and the mode of procedure the same. *Certain acts of Congress declared to be in force in the Indian country.* *To apply to fugitive slaves.*

SEC. 51. *And be it further enacted*, That if any person charged with a violation of any provision of this act, shall be found within any of the Confederate States, or any territory or province of the same, he s a be there apprehended and transported to the proper jurisdiction for trial. *Apprehension and transportation of persons to proper jurisdiction for trial.*

Protection against unlawful aggression or invasion.

SEC. 52. *And be it further enacted*, That each agent shall be empowered to protect citizens of the Confederate States, and members of any other Indian nation, peaceably and legally within the nation, for which he is agent, and not subject to its jurisdiction and laws, against any unlawful aggression upon or invasion of their rights, by individuals, or by the authorities of the nation. He shall have power

Removal of dangerous or improper persons.

to remove dangerous or improper persons, other than members of the nation by birth and blood, beyond the limits of the nation, subject only to an appeal to the superintendent; and to hear complaints of citizens

Reclamation of property, lost, strayed or stolen.

of the Confederate States, in reclamation of property lost, strayed or stolen, to examine testimony, and cause immediate restoration of such property, subject only to the like appeal to the superintendent, whose decision shall be final, saving the right of the parties to seek redress through the courts of competent jurisdiction. And for all these pur-

Military aid may be invoked.

poses the agent shall have power to call upon the commander of any military post for aid and assistance.

Power given agent to enforce the laws against the introduction of liquors.

SEC. 53. *And be it further enacted*, That each agent shall also have power to enforce the laws of the Confederate States, in regard to the introduction of spirituous liquors into the nations or tribes, for which he is agent, by seizure of the same, and apprehension and committment of the persons offending; to issue his warrant for the apprehension of such persons, and of persons charged with any other offence against the laws of the Confederate States, or of any State of the same; and to call to his assistance for the execution of the same, and of any warrant of commitment, or other process, for parties or witnesses, the troops of the Confederate States.

Armed police.

SEC. 54. *And be it further enacted*, That each agent may, with the approval of the superintendent, and when there are no troops of the Confederate States within his jurisdiction, keep in pay an armed police, composed of members of the nation or tribe, for which he is

Their number and compensation.

agent, not exceeding twenty-five in number, for such times and at such rate of compensation, as shall be sanctioned by the superintendent, whenever it may be necessary to preserve peace and order, or to enforce the laws of the Confederate States, by whom the expense of such police force shall be paid.

General duties of agents.

SEC. 55. *And be it further enacted*, That each agent shall be, within the limits of the country of the nation or tribes for which he is agent, *ex officio*, a commissioner in civil and criminal cases, of the courts of the Confederate States, with power and authority to take the testimony of witnesses, upon commission or otherwise; to administer oaths and receive affidavits; to cause to be apprehended persons charged with offences against the laws of the Confederate States, or of any State of the same, and found within his agency, to examine them and hear the witnesses, and thereupon to commit, bail or discharge the parties, and take recognizance of witnesses to appear at the proper time to testify; to perform all the duties of commissioner under the laws, for the rendition of fugitives from justice and fugitive slaves; to receive the authentication by oath, of accounts and claims against the Government, and all papers and pleadings needing to be sworn to in the courts of the Confederate States, and of all other papers whereto, by any regulation of any department of the Government, an oath or acknowledgment is required; and to perform the marriage ceremony, and to do and perform such other acts as a magistrate and notary public may do and perform, in any place under the sole and exclusive jurisdiction of the Confederate States; and may act as commissioner of any one or more of the Confederate States, to administer oaths, take depositions, and receive acknowledgments of deeds; and full faith and credit shall be given to all his acts and certificates, done and given within the purview of this act.

Sec. 56. *And be it further enacted,* That each agent shall be, *ex offi-* ·cio, ancillary administrator of all the goods and chattels, rights and credits, within his agency, of all citizens of the Confederate States, or persons, other than members of the nations or tribes, for which he is agent, who may die therein, with power to collect and take possession of the same, to sell such portions as may be perishable, and the rest to keep and preserve, and the whole to turn over and account for, to the regular administrator or executor in the proper jurisdiction.

To act as ancillary administrator.

Sec. 57. *And be it further enacted,* That for all services so perform-ed, each Agent shall receive from the parties, and the Confederate States, respectively, such fees as shall be fixed in the proper Courts, or by the regulations to be prescribed by the Secretary of War, or by the laws of the State, for which he may be commissioned; and shall re-ceive no other or larger fees or allowances, nor any gratuities whatever, under the penalty of being deemed guilty of corruption and extortion in office.

Fees for services.

Sec. 58. *And be it further enacted,* That the Secretary of War shall be, and he is hereby authorized and required to continue, adopt or pres-cribe such rules and regulations, as he may think fit, for carrying into effect, the various provisions of this act, and of any other act relating to Indian affairs, and for the settlement of the accounts of the Indian Bureau; and also such forms, as may be necessary or proper therefor; and when he shall have completely revised and arranged the same, to cause them to be printed in convenient form, and furnished to all offi-cers, and persons, who are to be governed or directed thereby. From the time of the promulgation whereof, all former rules and regulations in regard to Indian affairs, shall be deemed and taken to be rescinded.

Secretary of War, to prescribe certain rules and forms;

the same to be printed and distribu-ted.

Sec. 59. *And be it further enacted,* That all acts or parts of acts, contrary to the provisions of this act, are hereby repealed.

Laws repealed.

Approved April 8, 1862.

Chap. XX.—*An Act relative to the estimates of the heads of the several departments.*

April 9, 1862.

The Congress of the Confederate States of America do enact, That it shall be the duty of the heads of the several departments to com-municate to the Secretary of the Treasury the estimates of their re-spective departments thirty days prior to the assembling of Congress; and the Secretary of the Treasury shall submit said estimates, together with the estimates for his own department, to the President, ten days prior to the opening of the session of Congress.

Estimates of heads of departments to be communicated to Secretary of Treasu-ry.

Secretary to sub-mit same, with the estimates of his De-partment, to the President.

Sec. 2. *Be it further enacted,* That it shall be the duty of the seve-ral heads of departments, in case of estimates made during the session of Congress, to furnish the Secretary of the Treasury duplicates there-of, who shall report thereon to Congress the ways and means to pro-vide for the same.

Duplicates to be furnished Secretary, of estimates made during session of Con-gress.

Approved April 9, 1862.

Chap. XXI.—*An Act to authorise the advance of a certain sum of money to the State of Mis-souri.*

April 9, 1862.

The Congress of the Confederate States of America do enact, That the Secretary of the Treasury be authorised to issue to the State of Missouri the sum of one million of dollars, authorised by an act enti-

Advance of a cer-tain sum of money to the State of Missouri.

1862, Jan. 27.

tled an act for the relief of the State of Missouri, approved the 27th January, 1862, upon the authorised agent or -agents of said State, first filing with said Secretary the sum of four hundred and ninety-one thousand five hundred dollars, in bonds of said State of Missouri, as provided in said act, and executing a receipt for the remainder of such advance conditioned for the filing of the remainder of said amount in bonds of the State of Missouri, whenever the same can be conveniently done : *Provided*, Such remainder in bonds shall be filed with said Secretary within six months after the passage of this act.

Proviso.

Approved April 9, 1862.

April 10, 1862.

CHAP. XXII.—*An Act to provide for keeping all fire-arms in the armies of the Confederate States in the hands of effective men.*

Companies, &c., of troo s to be armed with pikes or other arms.

The Congress of the Confederate States of America do enact, That the President be, and he is hereby, authorised to organise companies, battalions or regiments of troops, to be armed with pikes, or other available arms, to be approved by him, when a sufficient number of arms of the kind now used in the service cannot be procured; such companies, battalions or regiments to be organised in the same manner as like organizations of infantry now are under existing laws.

How organized.

To serve as infantry or be attached to other regiments in the service.

Sec. 2. *Be it further enacted*, That the President may cause the troops armed and organised as herein provided, to serve as similar organizations of infantry now do, or to attach troops so armed to other regiments in the service, in numbers not exceeding two companies of troops so armed to each regiment. And the colonel of the regiment to which such companies may be attached, shall have power to detail men from such companies to take the place of men in the companies armed with fire-arms, whenever vacancies may occur from death, or discharge, or in cases of absence, from sickness, furlough, or any other cause; the true intent and meaning of this provision being to render every fire-arm in the army available at all times, by having it always in the hands of a well and effective man.

May be detailed to fill vacancies.

Secretary of War to furnish a copy of this act to every General in the service.

Sec. 3. Immediately after the passage of this act it shall be the duty of the Secretary of War to furnish a copy of the same to every General in the service.

Approved April 10, 1862.

April 10, 1862.

CHAP. XXIII.—*An Act to encourage enlistments in the corps of marines.*

Term of enlistment in the Marine corps.

The Congress of the Confederate States of America do enact, That from and after the passage of this act, enlistments in the marine corps shall be for the term of the existing war, or for the period of three years, as the recruit may elect at the time of enlistment.

Bounty.

Sec. 2. *Be it further enacted*, That every able-bodied man who may enlist and be received into the marine corps, shall be entitled to a bounty of fifty dollars, to be paid at the time of joining the corps, and every non-commissioned officer, musician and private, now in the marine corps, who may have enlisted for three years, shall be entitled to receive the sum of forty dollars, as an equivalent to bounty.

Sec. 3. *Be it further enacted*, That for the purpose of carrying into effect the provisions of this act, the sum of forty thousand dollars is hereby appropriated out of any money in the Treasury, not otherwise appropriated.

APPROVED April 10, 1862.

Appropriation.

CHAP. XXIV.—*An Act to legalize the Acts of the District Attorney, Marshal and Deputy Marshals of the State of Tennessee.*

April 11, 1862.

The Congress of the Confederate States of America do enact, That the official acts of J. G. Ramsey, late District Attorney, and of Jesse B. Clements, late Marshal of the District of Tennessee, and of the Deputies of said Marshal, from the time their respective offices were vacated, by the passage of the act of the Provisional Congress, approved on the twelfth day of December, 1861, by which said District of Tennessee was divided into three several districts, without any provision for continuing said officers in office, be, and the same are hereby, made legal and valid to the same extent and in the same manner, as if they had been continued in office up to the passage of this act; and they are hereby exonerated from any penalty, forfeiture or liability to the public or any private person by reason of any official act committed by them, to the same extent and in the same manner, as if they had been legally in office at the time of committing the same. And said officers are hereby authorised to collect and receive the same fees and emoluments as if they had been rightfully in office.

1861, Dec. 12. Official acts of the District Attorney, Marshal and Deputy Marshals of the State of Tennessee, legalized.

Fees and emoluments.

SEC. 2. *Be it further enacted,* That the said Marshal and his Deputies may continue to act until the successors of said Marshal are qualified.

Continuance of Marshal and his Deputies in office.

APPROVED April 11, 1862.

CHAP. XXV.—*An Act to authorize the Secretary of the Treasury to pay District Collectors in certain cases.*

April 11, 1862.

The Congress of the Confederate States of America do enact, That the Secretary of the Treasury be, and he is hereby, authorized to pay a part of the salaries of the several district collectors of the War tax, authorized by the act entitled " An Act to authorize the issue of Treasury notes and to provide a war tax for their redemption," approved August 19th, 1861, in those States which have assumed the payment of said tax: *Provided,* That in no case shall the amount so paid to each Collector exceed the sum of one hundred dollars: *And Provided, further,* The Secretary of the Treasury shall be satisfied that said collectors gave bond and rendered services as required by said act, previous to the assumption of said tax by the respective States, equal in value to the sum to be paid.

Payment of salaries to District Collectors of War Tax.

Maximum amount. Proviso.

APPROVED April 11, 1862.

CHAP. XXVI.—*An Act for the organization of a corps of officers for the working of nitre caves and establishing nitre beds.*

April 11, 1862.

The Congress of the Confederate States of America do enact, That for the purpose of procuring a supply of nitre, adequate to the wants of the Government, during the continuance of the war with the United States, the President be, and he is hereby, authorised to appoint a corps of officers, consisting of one superintendent, with the rank, pay and allowances of a major of artillery, four assistants, with the rank, pay and allowances of a captain of artillery, eight subordinates, with the rank, pay and allowances of first lieutenants of artillery.

Corps of officers for the working of nitre caves, etc.

Their duties.

SEC. 2. The duties of the officers, under the supervision of the Chief. of Ordnance, shall be to inaugurate and prosecute a system for the efficient working of the nitre caves, and to purchase and contract for the delivery of nitre produced within the limits of the Confederate States ; to inspect the nitre caves and other natural deposits of nitriferous earth, and to report the probable annual supply from these sources, and the extent and economy, or otherwise, with which they are now being worked by private enterprize ; to establish nitre beds in the vicinity of the principal cities and towns of the Confederacy, and to contract for the necessary grounds, sheds, etc., and for the offal and other materials used in the preparation of nitre beds ; to diffuse information and to stimulate enterprise in the production of an article essential to the success-

Superintendent to make report to Chief of Ordnance.

ful prosecution of the war. The superintendent will make reports, at stated periods, to the Chief of Ordnance, to be submitted to the Secre-

Organization ; how long to continue.

tary of War, for the information of Congress. This organization to be continued at the discretion of the President.

APPROVED April 11, 1862.

April 12, 1862.

CHAP. XXVII.—*An Act to provide further means for the support of the Government.*

1861, Aug. 19.
1861, Dec. 19.

The Congress of the Confederate States of America do enact, That the Secretary of the Treasury be, and he is hereby, authorised to issue, in addition to the amounts heretofore authorised to be issued by an act entitled "An Act to authorise the issue of Treasury notes and to provide a War Tax for their redemption," approved August 19th, 1861, and

Further issue of Treasury notes, certificates of stock and bonds, authorized.

by the further supplemental act to the above cited act, approved December 19th, 1861, from time to time, as the public necessities may require, Treasury notes, certificates of stock and bonds, not to exceed in the aggregate the sum of two hundred and fifteen millions of dollars, of which fifty millions shall be in Treasury notes, to be issued without reserve ; ten millions in Treasury notes to be used as a reserve fund, and to be issued to pay any sudden or unexpected call for deposits ; and one hundred and sixty-five millions certificates of stock or bonds: the said Treasury notes, certificates of stock and bonds to be issued under the same forms, conditions and restrictions as are provided by the above cited acts,

Secretary of the Treasury may effect loans.

in every respect and particular : *Provided, however,* That the Secretary of the Treasury may, if he shall deem the same advisable, effect a loan, at home or abroad, in specie funds or bills of exchange or Treasury notes, by a sale of the said bonds or stock upon such terms as may be found practicable : And *Provided, further,* That all bonds issued under

Bonds ; when redeemable.

this section shall be made redeemable at the pleasure of the Government after the expiration of ten years from their respective dates, but

Faith of the Government pledged.

the faith of the Government shall be pledged to redeem the same at the expiration of thirty years from such dates.

Bonds or certificates in exchange for Treasury notes.

SEC. 2. The Secretary of the Treasury may issue in exchange for any of the Treasury notes which may be issued under this or any other law, bonds or certificates, payable in not more than ten years, at a rate of interest not exceeding six per cent. per annum, payable semi-annually, to the extent of fifty millions of dollars, which fifty millions shall constitute part of the one hundred and sixty-five millions of stock and bonds

Reconvertible into Treasury notes.

above authorised ; the said bonds or certificates to be reconvertible, at the pleasure of the holder, into Treasury notes, and the said exchange and re-exchange to be subject to such regulations as the Secretary of the Treasury may prescribe.

Sec. 3. The form of the said bonds or certificates authorized by the second section above, shall be determined by the Secretary of the Treasury; the said certificates may be issued with or without coupons, and may be made payable to order or bearer, as may be deemed expedient.

Form.

May be with or without coupons.

Approved April 18, 1862.

Chap. XXVIII.—*An Act to increase the number of depositories of public funds.*

April 15, 1862.

The Congress of the Confederate States of America do enact, That the Secretary is hereby authorized to make and constitute such additional depositories of public moneys as in his judgment the public exigencies may require, which said depositaries shall give bond and be subject in all respects to the same laws and regulations, and be entitled to the same compensation as the depositories now authorized by law.

Additional depositaries of public moneys.

Depositaries to give bond.

Their compensation.

Sec. 2. The offices of the said additional depositories, appointed under this act, shall cease and determine at the expiration of one year after the termination of the existing war with the United States, unless otherwise ordered by Congress.

When their office to cease.

Approved April 15, 1862.

Chap. XXIX.—*An Act for the payment of musicians in the army, not regularly enlisted.*

April 15, 1862.

The Congress of the Confederate States of America do enact, That whenever colored persons are employed as musicians in any Regiment or Company, they shall be entitled to the same pay now allowed by law to musicians regularly enlisted: *Provided,* That no such persons shall be so employed except by the consent of the commanding officer of the Brigade to which said Regiments or Companies may belong.

Pay of colored persons employed as musicians.

Proviso.

Approved April 15, 1862.

Chap. XXX.—*An Act to amend An Act entitled "An Act to regulate the compensation of members of Congress," also to amend An Act entitled "An Act regulating the mode of paying members of Congress."*

April 16, 1862.

1862, March 25.
1862, March 26.

The Congress of the Confederate States of America do enact, That during the recess of Congress, the members of the Senate and House of Representatives are authorized to draw their drafts or orders on the Treasurer for their rateable monthly pay; and at the commencement of each session of Congress, the Treasurer shall report to each House the amount drawn by their respective members, during the preceding recess: *Provided* that the members of the Senate and House of Representatives, respectively, shall be entitled to draw their pay at the rate fixed by law up to the period of adjournment of each session.

Pay of members of Congress during recess of Congress.

Treasurer to report the amount drawn.

Approved April 16, 1862.

Chap. XXXI.—*An Act to further provide for the public defence.*

April 16, 1862.

In view of the exigencies of the country, and the absolute necessity of keeping in the service our gallant army, and of placing in the

Preamble.

field a large additional force to meet the advancing columns of the
enemy now invading our soil: Therefore

The Congress of the Confederate States of America do enact, That
the President be, and he is hereby authorized to call out and place in
the military service of the Confederate States, for three years, unless
the war shall have been sooner ended, all white men who are residents
of the Confederate States, between the ages of eighteen and thirty-
five years at the time the call or calls may be made, who are not legally exempted from military service. All of the persons aforesaid
who are now in the armies of the Confederacy, and whose term of
service will expire before the end of the war, shall be continued in the
service for three years from the date of their original enlistment, unless the war shall have been sooner ended: *Provided, however,* That
all such companies, squadrons, battalions, and regiments, whose term
of original enlistment was for twelve months, shall have the right,
within forty days, on a day to be fixed by the Commander of the Brigade, to re-organize said companies, battalions, and regiments, by elec-
ting all their officers, which they had a right heretofore to elect, who
shall be commissioned by the President : *Provided, further,* That furloughs not exceeding sixty days, with transportation home and back,
shall be granted to all those retained in the service by the provisions
of this Act beyond the period of their original enlistment, and who
have not heretofore received furloughs under the provisions of an Act
entitled "An Act providing for the granting of bounty and furloughs
to privates and non-commissioned officers in the Provisional Army,"
approved eleventh December, eighteen hundred and sixty-one, said furloughs to be granted at such times and in such numbers as the Secretary of War may deem most compatible with the public interest : and
Provided, further, That in lieu of a furlough the commutation value
in money of the transportation herein above granted, shall be paid to
each private, musician, or non-commissioned officer who may elect to
receive it, at such time as the furlough would otherwise be granted:
Provided, further, That all persons under the age of eighteen years or
over the age of thirty-five years, who are now enrolled in the military
service of the Confederate States, in the regiments, squadrons, battalions, and companies hereafter to be re-organized, shall be required to
remain in their respective companies, squadrons, battalions and regiments for ninety days, unless their places can be sooner supplied by
other recruits not now in the service, who are between the ages of
eighteen and thirty-five years ; and all laws and parts of laws providing for the re-enlistment of volunteers and the organization thereof into
companies, squadrons, battalions, or regiments, shall be and the same
are hereby repealed.

Sec. 2. *Be it further enacted;* That such companies, squadrons, battalions, or regiments organized, or in process of organization by authority from the Secretary of War, as may be within thirty days from the
passage of this Act, so far completed as to have the whole number of
men requisite for organization actually enrolled, not embracing in said
organizations any persons now in service, shall be mustered into the
service of the Confederate States as part of the land forces of the
same, to be received in that arm of the service in which they are authorized to organize, and shall elect their company, battalion, and regimental officers.

Sec. 3. *Be it further enacted,* That for the enrollment of all persons
comprehended within the provisions of this Act, who are not already
in service in the armies of the Confederate States, it shall be lawful
for the President, with the consent of the Governors of the respective

States, to employ State officers, and on failure to obtain such consent, he shall employ Confederate officers, charged with the duty of making such enrollment in accordance, with rules and regulations to be prescribed by him.

Sec. 4. *Be it further enacted*, That persons enrolled under the provisions of the preceding Section, shall be assigned by the Secretary of War, to the different companies now in the service, until each company is filled to its maximum number, and the persons so enrolled shall be assigned to companies from the States from which they respectively come. Persons enrolled assigned to companies in the service, from the States from which they come.

Sec. 5. *Be it further enacted*, That all Seamen and ordinary Seamen in the land forces of the Confederate States, enrolled under the provisions of this Act, may, on application of the Secretary of the Navy, be transferred from the land forces to the Naval service. Transfer of seamen from the land forces to the Naval service.

Sec. 6. *Be it further enacted*, That in all cases where a State may not have in the army a number of Regiments, Battalions, Squadrons or Companies, sufficient to absorb the number of persons subject to military service under this Act, belonging to such State, then the residue or excess thereof, shall be kept as a reserve, under such regulations as may be established by the Secretary of War, and that at stated periods of not greater than three months, details, determined by lot, shall be made from said reserve, so that each company shall, as nearly as practicable, be kept full: *Provided,* That the persons held in reserve may remain at home until called into service by the President: *Provided, also,* That during their stay at home, they shall not receive pay: *Provided, further,* That the persons comprehended in this Act, shall not be subject to the Rules and Articles of War, until mustered into the actual service of the Confederate States; except that said persons, when enrolled and liable to duty, if they shall wilfully refuse to obey said call, each of them shall be held to be a deserter, and punished as such, under said Articles: *Provided, further,* That whenever, in the opinion of the President, the exigencies of the public service may require it, he shall be authorized to call into actual service the entire reserve, or so much as may be necessary, not previously assigned to different companies in service under provision of section four of this Act; said reserve shall be organized under such rules as the Secretary of War may adopt: *Provided,* The company, battalion and regimental officers shall be elected by the troops composing the same: *Provided,* The troops raised in any one State shall not be combined in regimental, battalion, squadron or company organization with troops raised in any other States. Excess of enrolled persons kept as a reserve. Details from the reserve to keep each company to its maximum. Reserves may remain at home. Not to receive pay; nor be subject to rules and articles of war. When the entire reserve may be called into actual service. Organization. Election of officers. Troops raised in different States not to be combined.

Sec. 7. *Be it further enacted*, That all soldiers now serving in the army or mustered in the military service of the Confederate States, or enrolled in said service under the authorizations heretofore issued by the Secretary of War, and who are continued in the service by virtue of this Act, who have not received the bounty of fifty dolllars allowed by existing laws, shall be entitled to receive said bounty. Bounty.

Sec. 8. *Be it further enacted*, That each man who may hereafter be mustered into service, and who shall arm himself with a musket, shot-gun, rifle or carbine, accepted as an efficient weapon, shall be paid the value thereof, to be ascertained by the mustering officer under such regulations as may be prescribed by the Secretary of War, if he is willing to sell the same, and if he is not, then he shall be entitled to receive one dollar a month for the use of said received and approved musket, rifle, shot-gun or carbine. Pay for private arms.

Sec. 9. *Be it further enacted*, That persons not liable for duty may be received as substitutes for those who are, under such regulations as may be prescribed by the Secretary of War. Substitutes allowed.

Vacancies filled by promotion according to seniority.

Proviso.

SEC. 10. *Be it further enacted,* That all vacancies shall be filled by the President from the company, battalion, squadron or regiment in which such vacancies shall occur, by promotion according to seniority, except in case of disability or other incompetency : *Provided, however,* That the President may, when in his opinion, it may be proper, fill such vacancy or vacancies by the promotion of any officer or officers, or private or privates from such company, battalion, squadron or regiment who shall have been distinguished in the service by exhibition of valor and skill ; and that whenever a vacancy shall occur in the lowest grade of

Further proviso.

the commissioned officers of a company, said vacancy shall be filled by election : *Provided,* That all appointments made by the President shall be by and with the advice and consent of the Senate.

§1 of this Act to apply to certain regiments, &c.

SEC. 11. *Be it further enacted,* That the provisions of the first section of this Act, relating to the election of officers, shall apply to those regiments, battalions, and squadrons which are composed of twelve months and war companies combined in the same organization, without regard to the manner in which the officers thereof were originally appointed.

Complement of infantry ;

field artillery ;

cavalry.

SEC. 12. *Be it further enacted,* That each company of infantry shall consist of one hundred and twenty-five, rank and file ; each company of field artillery of one hundred and fifty, rank and file ; each of cavalry, of eighty, rank and file.

Persons subject to enrollment may volunteer.

SEC. 13. *Be it further enacted,* That all persons, subject to enrollment, who are not now in the service, under the provisions of this Act, shall be permitted, previous to such enrollment, to volunteer in companies now in the service.

APPROVED April 16, 1862.

April 17, 1862.

CHAP. XXXII.—*An Act to authorize the employment of Clerks at the offices of the Treasurer and Assistant Treasurers.*

WHEREAS, The issue and deposit of Treasury notes at the offices connected with the Treasury involve an increase of labor and responsibility : [Therefore]—

Secretary of the Treasury authorized to appoint additional Tellers and Book-keepers.

The Congress of the Confederate States of America do enact, That the Secretary of the Treasury is hereby authorized to employ such additional Tellers and Book-keepers as are required at the offices of the Treasurer and Assistant Treasurers for the additional duties required

Compensation.

in the receipt and disbursement of Treasury notes : *Provided* the compensation to be allowed shall not exceed the rate of twelve hundred dollars *per annum,* for each Teller or Clerk : and *Provided also,* that

Number.

the number of Clerks to be employed shall not exceed seven : and, *Provided,* that no person shall be appointed in either of said offices who is under the age of forty years, and capable of active service in

Proviso.

the army : and, *Provided, further,* that a preference shall, in all cases, be given, in making appointments, the qualifications being equal, to those who have been discharged from the military service of the country on account of wounds received, or disease contracted, in the line of duty.

APPROVED April 17, 1862.

April 17, 1862

CHAP. XXXIII.—*An Act to authorize the Secretary of War to divide the appropriation for the contingent expenses of the War Department and the Army.*

Secretary of War to divide appropriations for the contingent expenses of the Army and War Department.

The Congress of the Confederate States of America do enact, That the appropriation of two hundred thousand dollars made for the incidental and contingent expenses of the Army and of the War Department, in the Act entitled "An Act making appropriations for the support of the Government from April first to the thirteenth of November eighteen hundred and sixty-two," approved April third, eighteen hundred and sixty-two, be divided and applied, by the Secretary of War, to the incidental and contingent expenses of the War Department and to those of the Army, in such proportions, as, in his opinion, the exigencies of the public service may require.

APPROVED April 17, 1862.

1862, April 8.

CHAP. XXXIV.—*An Act to encourage the manufacture of Saltpetre and of Small Arms.*   April 17, 1862.

The Congress of the Confederate States of America do enact, That any person or persons who may propose to establish within the limits of the Confederate States a manufactory or manufactories of Saltpetre and of Small Arms adapted to the use of the army, shall be entitled to receive from the Government an advance of fifty per cent. of the amount required for the erection and preparation of the works and machinery necessary to such manufactory or manufactories, to be repaid without interest in the product of such manufactory or manufactories, at a price to be agreed upon before such advance shall be made, and subject to the following conditions, to wit:—First, That the contractor or contractors shall submit to the President a plan of the proposed works, showing their location, nature and extent, together with a sworn estimate of their probable cost, and a detailed account under oath of the amount already expended on the same, which amount shall be at least twenty-five per cent. of the entire estimated cost of such work. Second, That the amount so advanced shall be paid in instalments as the works shall progress towards completion. Third, That the proposed enterprise and works shall be approved by the President. Fourth, That the contractor or contractors shall enter into bond with sufficient security, to be approved by the President, in the penalty of double the amount proposed to be advanced, and conditioned that the principal obligor or obligors shall well and truly, by a certain time, (which may be extended by the President if he thinks proper,) named in the bond, proceed to erect, complete and put into effective operation the manufactory or manufactories proposed; that he or they will expend the sum named for these purposes; that he or they will appropriate the money advanced by the Government to such purpose and to no other use or purpose, and, as far as practicable, keep the property insured; and that he or they will repay the same from the merchantable articles manufactured, to be delivered at such times and in such quantities as may be agreed upon, the same, in all cases, to be inspected by a government officer before it is received, until he or they shall fully repay to the Confederate States, in the article and at the price stipulated for the sum advanced; that the contractor or contractors shall subscribe a written oath, endorsed upon the back of said bond, which may be administered by any one authorized to administer an oath, that said advance is asked for the purposes specified in this Act, and no other, and that he or they will so apply said funds, which may thus be advanced; and a willful and corrupt violation of this oath shall be deemed perjury, and punishable by imprisonment for not less than three nor more than ten years.

SEC. 2. The provisions of this Act shall apply to cases of enlargement or manufactories of Saltpetre and of Small Arms, now established of being established within the Confederate States, but the advances made in such cases, shall only be fifty per cent. upon the

Manufactories of Saltpetre and of Small Arms.

Advances by the Government.

Plan of the works.

Advances payable in instalments.

President's approval.

Contractors to give bond.

Penalty.

Condition.

Oath.

Penalty for perjury.

This Act to apply to cases of enlargement of existing manufactories.

3

amount proposed to be invested in the enlargement of such manufactory or manufactories; and no now existing investment in such manufactory or manufactories shall be computed or taken into account in determining such fifty per cent.

APPROVED April 17, 1862.

April 17, 1862.

CHAP. XXXV.—*An Act authorizing the issue of Treasury Notes.*

Issue of Treasury Notes of the denomination of one and two dollars.

The Congress of the Confederate States of America do enact, That in addition to the Treasury Notes, authorized to be issued under previous acts, the Secretary of the Treasury is hereby required to prepare and put in circulation, by such means as he may deem proper to adopt, five millions of dollars of Treasury Notes of the Confederate States, of the denomination of one dollar and two dollars. Said notes shall be issued in such proportions of each, to the aggregate sum herein authorized as the said Secretary may determine, payable to bearer, six months after the ratification of a treaty of peace, between the Confederate States and the United States. Said notes shall be receivable in payment of all public dues, including postage, except the export duty on cotton.

When Payable.

Receivable in payment of public dues except &c.

Printing of the notes.

SEC. 2. *Be it further enacted,* That the Secretary is hereby authorized to have said notes printed as he may deem most practicable and advisable in effecting a speedy issue and circulation of said notes.

Issue of Treasury Notes of not less than $100, bearing interest.

SEC. 3. *Be it further enacted,* That the Secretary of the Treasury is hereby authorized to issue Treasury notes payable in six months after the ratification of a treaty of peace, between the Confederate States and the United States, of a denomination not less than one hundred dollars, bearing interest at the rate of two cents per day for each hundred dollars; the said notes when issued to be a substitute for so much of the one hundred and sixty-five millions of bonds authorized by the act of Congress, passed at the present session; and said notes shall be receivable in payment of all public dues except the export duty on cotton.

To be a substitute for certain bonds.

Receivable in payment of all dues, except, &c.

Report by Secretary to Congress.

SEC. 4. *Be it further enacted,* That the said Secretary shall make report to Congress of the amount of each denomination of notes, herein required to be issued, which he may put in circulation.

Act of 1861, Aug. 19, §§ 21 and 23, against the forgery of notes, &c., to apply.

SEC. 5. *Be it further enacted,* That the twenty-first and twenty-third sections of "An act to authorize the issue of Treasury Notes, and to provide a War Tax for their redemption" be, and the same are hereby declared to apply to the Treasury Notes herein authorized, as fully, in all respects, as if the same constituted a part of this act.

APPROVED April 17, 1862.

April 19, 1862.

CHAP. XXXVI.—*An Act to aid in the construction of a certain line of railroad in the States of Louisiana and Texas.*

Preamble.

WHEREAS, The Confederate States are engaged in actual war, and the President has recommended, for military reasons, the construction of the railroad from New Iberia, in the State of Louisiana, and Houston, in the State of Texas, and the Commanding General at New Orleans has declared it to be at the present moment a great military necessity: [Therefore—]

Construction of railroad from New Iberia, Louisiana, and Houston, Texas.

Contract for the completion and connection of said roads.

The Congress of the Confederate States of America do enact, That the President be, and he is *he is* hereby authorized and empowered to aid or contract with the New Orleans and Texas Railroad Company, and the Texas and New Orleans Railroad Company, upon such terms and conditions as he may think proper, to insure the prompt completion and connection of said roads, in the manner he may think best calculated to promote the public interest.

SEC. 2. *Be it further enacted,* That to enable the President to accomplish the object herein contemplated, the sum of one million five hundred thousand dollars in the bonds of the Confederate States, is hereby appropriated to be issued and applied by the order of the President at such times and in such sums as he may deem proper, and that the President be directed to take a mortgage on said road and its appurtenances for the ultimate repayment of the money so expended in aid of its erection. *Appropriation.*

Mortgage on the road.

APPROVED April 19, 1862.

CHAP. XXXVII.—*An Act to repeal certain laws therein named and to declare others in full force, in relation to conveyance of mailable matter outside of the mail.* April 19, 1862.

The Congress of the Confederate States of America do enact, That so much of the existing enactments of the Confederate States, as relates to the conveyance or transportation of letters or packages of letters or of mailable matter of any kind by express or other companies of any kind, their agents or employees, be and the same are hereby repealed, and the laws of the United States adopted by an act of the Provisional Congress entitled "An Act to continue in force certain laws of the United States of America," on the ninth day of February, one thousand, eight hundred and sixty-one, relating to the conveyance or transportation of letters, packets, or packages of letters or other mailable matter by express or other companies, their agents or employees, be and the same are hereby declared to be in full force : *Provided,* That nothing in this act contained shall be so construed as to declare that any portion of said laws of the United States, adopted as aforesaid, not inconsistent with the acts of the said Provisional Government was by said last named acts in any wise abrogated or repealed : *Provided, further,* That frauds upon the revenue of the Post Office Department and offences against and violations of the laws hereby repealed may be proceeded against and punished under the laws existing at the time of the commission of such fraud, offence or violation, and this act shall not be construed to have a retroactive operation so as to repeal or abrogate any law as to such frauds, offences or violations heretofore committed, but shall have a prospective operation only : *Provided, also,* That this act shall take effect from and after the first of June, one thousand, eight hundred and sixty-two.

Certain laws repealed and others declared in force, relating to the conveyance of mailable matter by express or other companies.

1861, Feb. 9.

Proviso.

Frauds upon the revenue of the P. O. Department, how punished.

How this act to be construed.

When to take effect.

APPROVED April 19, 1862.

CHAP. XXXVIII.—*An Act regulating the fees of Marshals and for other purposes.* April 19, 1862.

The Congress of the Confederate States of America do enact, That all laws now in force prescribing the fees of Marshals of the Confederate States be, and the same are hereby repealed ; and in lieu thereof the said Marshals shall be allowed to have and charge the fees following, to wit :

For service of any warrant, attachment, summons, capias or other writ (except execution, venire or summons, or subpœna for a witness,) two dollars for each person on whom such service may be made : *Marshals' fees.*

Provided, That, on petition setting forth the facts on oath, 'the court may allow such fair compensation for the keeping of personal property, attached and held on mesne process, as shall, on examination, be found to be reasonable.

For serving a writ of subpœna on a witness, fifty cents; and no further compensation shall be allowed for any copy, summons or notice for witness.

For travel in going to serve any process, warrant, attachment, or other writ, including writs of subpœna in civil and criminal cases, five cents per mile for going and the same for returning, to be computed from the court where the process is issued, to the place where served, by the route usually travelled between such points; and if more than one person is served therewith, the travel shall be computed from the court to the place of service which shall be most remote, adding thereto the extra travel which shall be necessary to serve it on the other. And in all cases where mileage is allowed to the Marshal by this Act, it shall be at his option to receive the same, or his actual traveling expenses, to be proved on his oath to the satisfaction of the court.

For each bail bond, fifty cents.

For summoning appraisers, each, fifty cents. For every commitment or discharge of a prisoner, fifty cents.

For every proclamation in admiralty, thirty cents. For sales of vessels or other property, under process in admiralty, or under the order of a court of admiralty, and for receiving and paying the money, one per centum on the amount.

For serving an attachment *in rem*, or a libel in admiralty, two dollars; and the necessary expenses of keeping boats, vessels or other property attached or libelled in admiralty to be ascertained and allowed by the court.

For serving a writ of possession, partition, execution, or any final process, the same mileage as is herein allowed for the service of any other writ: *Provided*, That no charge for mileage in any case shall be made, except for the distance actually travelled; and for making the service, seizing or levying on property; advertising and disposing of the same by sale, set-off or otherwise, according to law, receiving and paying over the money, the same fees, commissions and poundage, as are or shall be allowed for similar service to the Sheriffs of the several States, respectively, in which the service may be rendered.

For serving venires, and summoning jurors, fifty cents each: *Provided*, That, in no case shall the fees for distributing and serving venires, and summoning jurors, including mileage chargeable by the Marshal for such service, at any court, exceed fifty dollars.

For traveling from his residence to the place of holding court, to attend a term thereof, ten cents per mile for going and the same for returning, and five dollars per day for attending the court and for bringing in and committing prisoners and witnesses during the term.

For executing a deed prepared by a party or his attorney, one dollar.

For drawing and executing a deed, five dollars.

For transporting criminals to the Penitentiary, or other place of confinement, ten cents per mile for each necessary guard and each prisoner, for going only, and ten cents per mile for himself for going and returning.

For conveying prisoners under arrest from the place of arrest to the court where the prisoners are to be tried, ten cents per mile for himself and each necessary guard, and each prisoner.

For copies of writs or papers furnished at the request of any party, ten cents per folio.

For holding a Court of Enquiry, or other proceedings before a jury, including the summoning of a jury, five dollars.

For attending examinations before a commissioner and bringing in, guarding and returning persons charged with crime, five dollars per day for himself, and three dollars per day for each deputy necessarily attending, not exceeding two.

The respective courts of the Confederate States shall appoint criers for their courts, to be allowed the sum of two dollars per day; and the Marshals are hereby authorized to appoint such a number of persons, not exceeding five, as the Judges of their respective Courts shall determine, to attend upon the Grand and other Juries, and for other necessary purposes, who shall be allowed for their services the sum of two dollars per day, to be paid by, and included in the accounts of the Marshal, out of any money of the Confederate States in his hands; the compensation to be given only for actual attendance. *Criers and persons attending on juries.*

For expenses while employed in endeavoring to arrest, under process, any person charged with or convicted of a crime, the sum actually expended, not to exceed two dollars per day, in addition to his compensation for service and travel. *Marshals allowed certain expenses.*

For disbursing money to jurors and witnesses and for other expenses, two per centum. *Allowance for disbursing money.*

SEC. 2. *And be it further enacted,* That there shall be paid to the Marshal his fees for services rendered for the Confederate States for summoning jurors and witnesses in behalf of the Confederate States, and in behalf of any prisoner to be tried for any capital offence; for the maintenance of prisoners of the Confederate States, confined in jail for any criminal offence; for the commitment or discharge of such prisoners; for the expenses necessarily incurred for fuel, lights and other contingencies, that may accrue in holding the Courts within the District, and providing the books necessary to record the proceedings thereof: *Provided,* That the Marshal shall not incur an expense of more than twenty dollars in any one year for furniture, or fifty dollars for rent of building and making improvements thereon, without first submitting a statement and estimates to the Department of Justice and getting instructions in the premises. *Fees to be paid to Marshals for services rendered the Confederate States.* *Contingent expenses.* *Proviso.*

SEC. 3. *And be it further enacted,* That in lieu of the compensation now allowed to jurors in the Confederate Courts, by virtue of the twenty-fifth section of the Act to establish the Judicial Courts of the Confederate States of America, passed March sixteenth, eighteen hundred and sixty-one, there be hereafter allowed to such jurors two dollars per day while in actual attendance on any of such courts, and for travelling from their residence to said courts, five cents per mile for going and the same for returning. *1861, March 16.* *Allowance to jurors.*

SEC. 4. *And be it further enacted,* That in lieu of the compensation now allowed by law to witnesses summoned in behalf of the Confederate States, they shall be allowed one dollar and fifty cents for each day's attendance in court, or before any officer pursuant to law, and five cents per mile for travelling from their places of residence to said place of trial or hearing, and five cents per mile for returning. *To witnesses.*

APPROVED April 19, 1862.

CHAP. XXXIX.—*An Act making further appropriations for the expenses of the Government in the Treasury, War and Navy Departments, and for other purposes.* April 19, 1862.

The Congress of the Confederate States of America do enact, That the following sums be, and they are hereby appropriated out of any money in the Treasury not otherwise appropriated, for the objects here- *Further appropriations for the year ending Nov. 30, 1862.*

after expressed, for the year ending November thirtieth, one thousand eight hundred and sixty-two:

Treasury Department.

Treasury Department.—For additional clerks to be employed in the offices of the Treasurer, Asssistant Treasurers and Depositaries of the Confederate States, five thousand six hundred dollars.

Miscellaneous.

Miscellaneous.—For the interest on the public debt, nine millions of dollars. For paper, plates and printing an additional amount of bonds and large Treasury notes, one hundred thousand dollars. For eight additional clerks required for issue of bonds and coupons, four thousand dollars. For paper, plates and printing of Treasury notes of the denominations of one and two dollars, seventy-five thousand dollars. For twelve additional clerks to sign small Treasury notes, six thousand dollars.

War Department.

War Department.—For the purchase of pig and rolled iron, one million of dollars. For casting cannon, shot and shells, five hundred thousand dollars. For manufacturing small arms of all kinds, two millions of dollars. For purchase and manufacture of nitre and all expenses incidental to exploring and working caves, &c., one million of dollars.

Navy Department.

Navy Department.—To make advances on contracts for the manufacture and production of iron, one million of dollars. For the purchase by the Secretary of the Treasury of exchange for the use of the Navy Department, in purchasing iron clad vessels, one million four hundred thousand dollars.

APPROVED April 19, 1862.

April 19, 1862.

CHAP. XL.—*An Act to organize a Signal Corps.*

Signal Corps.

The Congress of the Confederate States of America do enact, That the President be and is hereby authorized by and with the advice and consent of the Senate, to appoint ten officers in the Provisional Army, of a grade not exceeding that of Captains, and with the pay of corresponding grades of *Infantry,* who shall perform the duties of Signal Officers of the Army. And the President is hereby authorized to appoint ten Sergeants of *Infantry,* in the Provisional Army, and to assign them to duty as Signal Sergeants. The Signal Corps above authorized may be organized as a separate corps, or may be attached to the Department of the Adjutant and *Inspector* General, or to the Engineer Corps, as the Secretary of War shall direct.

APPROVED April 19, 1862.

April 19, 1862.

CHAP. XLI.—*An Act supplementary to the Act entitled "An Act to encourage the manufacture of Saltpetre and Small Arms."*

1862, April 17.

The Congress of the Confederate States of America do enact, That the provisions of the act entitled "An Act to encourage the manufacture of Saltpetre and of Small Arms," shall also apply to all establish-

Coal and Iron mines.

ments or mines for the production of coal and for the production and manufacture of iron, and that in addition to the advance of fifty per cent. therein mentioned, the President be and he is, hereby authorized

Contracts for the purchase of Coal and Iron.

to enter into contracts for the purchase of coal and iron, in such quantities as may probably be required for a series of years, not exceeding six, and to make advances thereon not exceeding one-third of the amount of such contract.

APPROVED April 19, 1862.

The Congress of the Confederate States of America do enact, That Post Routes estab-lished: the following post routes be and the same are hereby established, to wit:

In the *State of Alabama.*—From Guntersville, by way of Larkins- *In Alabama..* ville, on the Memphis and Charleston Railroad, to Bellefonte. From Syliacogga to I. I. Richards, in Coosa County.

In the *State of Arkansas.*—From Parks to Blackfork, in Scott coun- *In Arkansas.* ty. From Jacksonport, by Black and Current Rivers, to Cherokee Point, in Randolph county. From Trenton, by Hickory Grove to Clarendon. From Camden by way of El Dorado, in Union county, to Monroe, in the State of Louisiana. From Washington to Hempstead county, by way of Nashville, Ozan Post Office, Wilton and Murfreesboro' to Roys-ton, in Pike county. From Warren, by way of Johnsville, to Ham-burgh.

In the *State of Florida.*—From Waldo Station, on the Florida Rail- *In Florida.* road, to Etoriah.

In the *State of Georgia.*—From Athens, by way of Harmony Grove *In Georgia.* and Phi Delta, to Homer. From Lebeauville, on the Savannah, Al-bany and Gulf Railroad, to Waresboro'. From Athens to Lawrence-ville. From Harmony Grove, by way of Homer and Webb's Creek, to Hollingsworth. From Nesota, Baker county, to Camilla.

In the *State of Louisiana.*—From Natchetoches, on Red River, to *In Louisiana.* Monroe, on the Ouachita River.

In the *State of Mississippi.*—From Lake Station, by way of Pine- *In Mississippi.* ville, to Flover's Place, in Smith county.

In the *State of Tennessee.*—From Cade's Cave to Mont Vale Springs. *In Tennessee.* From Cookville to Gainesboro'.

In the *State of Virginia.*—From Arrington, by way of Massie's Mills, *In Virginia.* to Tye River Mills, in Nelson county.

In the *State of North Carolina.*—From Slatesville, by way of Tay- *In North Carolina.* lorsville, Wilkesboro' and Jefferson, to Marion, in the State of Vir-ginia.

In the *State of South Carolina.*—From Simsville, by way of Maybur- *In South Carolina.* ton, to Goshen Hill.

In *North Carolina.*—From Franklin, North Carolina, to Walhalla, in *In North Carolina.* South Carolina.

In the *State of Texas.*—From Hookley's Depot, on the Houston and *In Texas.* Central Railroad, to Waller's Store. From Hickory Station, in Cataw-ba county, North Carolina, to Lenoir.

Approved April 19, 1862.

Chap. XLIII.—*An Act to increase the Military Establishment of the Confederate States, and*   April 19, 1862.
to amend the "Act for the establishment and organization of the Army of the Confederate States
of America."

The Congress of the Confederate States of America do enact, That Number of Ord-nance Sergeants in-creased. the number of Ordnance Sergeants authorized by section six of "An Act to increase the Military Establishment of the Confederate States," &c., approved May 16th, 1861, be so increased as to provide one for *1861, May 16.* each regiment of the troops now or hereafter received in the service.

Approved April 19, 1862.

April 19, 1862.

CHAP. XLIV.—*An Act to limit the Act authorizing the suspension of the Writ of Habeas Corpus.*

Act suspending writ of habeas corpus, defined.

The Congress of the Confederate States of America do enact, That the act authorizing the suspension of the writ of habeas corpus, is hereby limited to arrests made by the authorities of the Confederate Government, or for offences against the same.

How long said act to continue in force.

SEC. 2. *Be it further enacted,* That the act which this act is intended to limit shall continue in force for thirty days after the next meeting of Congress, and no longer.

APPROVED April 19, 1862.

April 19, 1862.

CHAP. XLV.—*An Act to amend An Act entitled "An Act to prescribe the Rates of Postage in the Confederate States of America, and for other purposes"*

Rates of postage on letters.

The Congress of the Confederate States of America do enact, That from and after the first day of July next, there shall be charged the following rates of postage, to wit: For every single letter sealed, and for every letter in manuscript or paper of any kind, upon which information shall be asked for, or communicated in writing, or by marks or signs, conveyed in the mails for any distance within the Confederate States of America, ten cents; and every letter or parcel not exceeding half an ounce in weight, shall be deemed a single letter, and every additional half ounce, or additional weight of less than half an ounce, shall be charged with an additional single postage.

What deemed a single letter.

Additional single postage.

APPROVED April 19, 1862.

April 19, 1862.

CHAP. XLVI.—*An Act to authorize the employment of Drill Masters.*

Drill Masters.

The Congress of the Confederate States of America do enact, That the President be and he is hereby authorized and empowered to appoint Drill Masters for Camps of Instruction or reserve forces in any arm of the military service, with such pay as the Secretary of War may prescribe.

APPROVED April 19, 1862.

April 19, 1862.

CHAP. XLVII.—*An Act in relation to Auditing Accounts for the War Department.*

Auditing Accounts for the War Department.

The Congress of the Confederate States of America do enact, That it shall be the duty of the Second Auditor, after examining the accounts for the War Department, to certify the balances and transmit the account with the vouchers and certificates to the Comptroller for his decision thereon, and when finally adjusted, said accounts, vouchers and certificates shall be filed with the Register, as required by the act "to establish the Treasury Department," approved February twenty-first, eighteen hundred and sixty-one.

1861, Feb. 21.

APPROVED April 19, 1862.

April 19, 1862.

CHAP. XLVIII.—*An Act to amend "An Act to regulate the mode of paying the members of the Senate and House of Representatives, and the disbursement of the Contingent Fund."*

1862, March 26.

The Congress of the Confederate States of America do enact, That the compensation due to the officers of the Senate shall be certified by the Secretary of the Senate, at such times as *is* provided by law, and the Sergeant-at-Arms shall draw upon the Treasury for the amounts thus certified, and the drafts shall be paid from the Treasury of the Confederate States when issued according to law.

Compensation due officers of the Senate;

by whom certified and how paid.

Sec. 2. That the compensation due to the officers of the House of Representatives shall be certified to by the Clerk of said House, at such times as *is* provided by law; and the said Clerk shall draw upon the Treasury for the amounts thus certified, and the drafts shall be paid from the Treasury of the Confederate States, when issued according to law.

Compensation due officers of the House;

by whom certified and how paid.

Approved April 19, 1862.

Chap. XLIX.—*An Act to limit the compensation of Clerks, Marshals and District Attorneys of the Confederate States.*   April 19, 1862.

The Congress of the Confederate States of America do enact, That every District Attorney, Clerk of a District Court and Marshal of the Confederate States shall, until otherwise directed by law, upon the first day of January and July in each year, commencing with the first day of July next or within thirty days from and after the days specified, make to the Attorney General, in such form as he shall prescribe, a return in writing, embracing all the fees and emoluments of their respective offices of every name and character, distinguishing the fees and emoluments received or payable under the Sequestration Acts from those received or payable for any other service ; and in the case of a Marshal further distinguishing the fees and emoluments received or payable for services by himself personally rendered from those received or payable for services rendered by a deputy : and also embracing all necessary office expenses of such officers, the necessary clerk hire included, to be verified by the oath of the officer making the same. And no District Attorney shall be allowed to retain of the fees and emoluments of his said office, for his own personal compensation, over and above his necessary office expenses, the necessary clerk hire included, to be audited and allowed by the proper accounting officers of the Treasury, a sum exceeding five thousand dollars per year, and at and after that rate for such time as he shall hold the office ; and no Clerk of a District Court shall be allowed to retain of the fees and emoluments of his office for his own personal compensation, over and above the necessary expenses of his office, the necessary clerk hire included, to be audited and allowed by the proper officers of the Treasury a sum exceeding four thousand dollars per year, or at and after that rate for such time as he shall hold his office. And no Marshal shall be allowed to retain of the fees and emoluments of his office, for his own personal compensation over and above a proper allowance to his deputies, which shall in no case exceed three-fourths of the fees and emoluments received as payable for the services rendered by the deputy to whom this allowance is made, and over and above the necessary office expenses of such Marshal, necessary clerk hire included, also to be audited and allowed by the proper accounting officer of the Treasury, a sum exceeding five thousand dollars per year, or at and after that rate for such time as he shall hold office; and every such officer shall with each such return made by him pay into the Treasury of the Confederate States, or deposit to the credit of the Treasurer thereof, any surplus of the fees and emoluments of his office, which his half-yearly return so made shall show to exist over and

District Attorneys, Clerks of District Courts and Marshals, to make returns in writing, semi-annually, to the Attorney General.

Maximum Compensation allowed District Attorneys,

Clerks of District Courts,

and Marshals,

Surplus of fees, etc., to be paid into the Public Treasury.

above the compensation and allowances herein authorized to he retained and paid by him.

Approved April 19, 1862.

April 19, 1862.

Chap. L.—*An Act to provide for the appointment of Chaplains at the Naval Hospitals.*

Chaplains to the Naval Hospitals.

The Congress of the Confederate States of America do enact, That the President may, in his discretion, appoint and assign to the Naval Hospitals in the Confederate States, Chaplains, for service during the continuance of the existing war, who shall receive the same pay and emoluments as Chaplains in the Army.

Pay.

Approved April 19, 1862.

April 19, 1862.

Chap. LI.—*An Act to regulate the collection of the War Tax in certain States invaded by the Enemy.*

1861, Aug. 19.

The Congress of the Confederate States of America do enact, That where any State has assumed, or shall assume, the payment of the tax imposed by the act entitled an act to authorize the issue of Treasury Notes, and to provide a War Tax for their redemption, approved the nineteenth day of August, eighteen hundred and sixty-one, and any portion of such State shall be occupied by the enemy, so as to occasion the destruction of crops, or prevent the raising thereof, or to prevent the State from collecting taxes therein, the President may, under an agreement with the State authorities of such States, suspend the payment into the Treasury of such portions of the tax assumed by such State as may have been, or may be, assessed upon the property of the inhabitants of such districts so occupied by the enemy, until further provision be made by Congress.

Payment of War Tax, by States that have assumed the payment thereof, suspended, so far as assessed on property in districts invaded by the enemy.

Collection of War Tax in Missouri and Kentucky, suspended.

Sec. 2. The suspension of all proceedings in relation to the collection of the War Tax in the States of Missouri and Kentucky, authorized by the Secretary of the Treasury, is confirmed, and he is hereby directed to take no action thereon until further legislation by Congress.

Approved April 19, 1862.

April 19, 1862.

Chap. LII.—*An Act regulating the fees of Clerks and for other purposes.*

Clerks' fees.

The Congress of the Confederate States of America do enact, That all laws now in force prescribing the fees of Clerks of the Courts of said Confederate States be and the same are hereby repealed, and that in lieu thereof the said clerks shall be allowed to have and charge as follows, to wit:

For issuing and entering every process, commission, summons, subpœna in chancery, capias, notice or garnishee summons, under the Sequestration Act, warrant, attachment, or other writ, except a subpœna for a witness, one dollar: *Provided,* That for all summons of garnishment arising under the Sequestration Acts, the clerk shall be allowed only twenty-five cents.

For issuing a subpœna for a witness, or witnesses if more than one be named in the same subpœna, twenty-five cents.

For filing and entering every declaration, plea, or demurrer, whether written or not, or other written paper in any suit, for each, ten cents.

For administering every oath or affirmation to a witness or other person, except a juror, ten cents.

For entering the return on any process when proper to do so, fifteen cents.

For every rule entered in the rule book on one rule day, twenty-five cents.

For any order, continuance, judgment, decree or recognizance, drawing any bond or making any record, certificate return or report, for every one hundred words fifteen cents, or a specific fee of forty cents.

For a copy of any such entry or record, or any other record or paper, for every one hundred words ten cents, or a specific fee of twenty cents.

For entering in any suit or controversy in Court, all the attorneys for each party, or the appearance in proper person of any party having no attorney who appears, ten cents.

For making dockets and indexes and for other services for which no specific fee is allowed on the trial or argument of a cause, where issue is joined and testimony given, including venire and taxing costs, three dollars.

For making dockets and indexes and for other services for which no specific fee is allowed in a cause where issue is joined and no testimony given, including taxing costs, two dollars.

For making dockets and indexes, and for taxing costs and other services, for which no particular fee is allowed in a cause which is dismissed or a judgment or decree is rendered therein without issue, including taxing costs, one dollar.

For affixing the seal of Court to any instrument, when required, or to any process to which the same is required to be affixed by law, twenty cents.

For every search, for anything above a year's standing, except where such search is for papers in a pending cause, twenty cents.

For noting in the process book any decree, order or process, (except a subpœna for a witness,) and taking a receipt therefor, twenty cents.

For recording a bond or other writing in pursuance of an order of Court, for every one hundred words, fifteen cents, or a specific fee of one dollar.

Where a witness claims for his attendance, for administering an oath to him, and entering and certifying such attendance, forty cents.

For administering any oath not before provided for, and writing a certificate thereof, where the case requires one, fifty cents.

For receiving, keeping and paying out money, in pursuance of the requirements of any statute or order of Court, one per cent. on the amount so received, kept and paid.

For attendance on Court when the same is actually in session, for each day five dollars.

For travelling from the office of the clerk, where he is required by law to reside, or where he actually does reside, to the place of holding any court required to be held by law, five cents per mile for going and the same for returning. Mileage.

The said fees shall be chargeable to the party at whose instance the service is performed, except that fees for entering and certifying the attendance of witnesses, and the proceedings to compel payment for such attendance, shall be charged to the party for whom the witness attended, and the per diem, mileage and other service performed for the Government of the Confederate States, shall be paid by said Government. All fees which may accrue to the clerk under the Sequestration Act, or any act amendatory thereof, by law chargeable on said To whom fees, etc., are charged.
Fees under Sequestration Act, how paid.

fund, shall be paid out of the general sequestered fund in the hands of any receiver, or under the control of the Court, when an order shall be made directing such payment, and the Court is authorized to make such order at its discretion. No person shall be compelled to

Fee bills, how made out. pay any fees before mentioned until a fee bill be produced to him, signed by the clerk to whom they are due, expressing the particulars for which such fees are charged; and the said fee bills made out and

To whom fee bills are delivered for collection; power and duty of collecting officer. signed as aforesaid, the clerk may deliver to the marshal or to a sheriff of the State where the party resides, who shall collect the same, deducting a commission of ten per cent. for such collection, and the marshal or sheriff may distrain therefor such property of the person to whom the fees are charged as might be levied on under a writ of fieri facias issued from a State court of the said respective Confederate States; and the District Courts of the Confederate States shall, on

How fee bill may be quashed. motion, and for good cause shown, quash any such fee bill and prevent the collection thereof, or of so much thereof as appears to be illegal and not justly due. No clerk shall be obliged to perform services for a non-resident of the district for which he is clerk, unless payment of

When clerk is entitled before performing services to have security for his fees. his fees for said services be secured, nor to perform services for any person against whom he has had a fee bill returned, and which remains unsatisfied, unless he be secured payment of his fees for the services desired, or performance of said services be directed by the court.

Record books and stationery. SEC. 2. *And the Congress of the Confederate States do further enact,* That all necessary record books and stationery shall be furnished the said clerks at the cost of the Government, and that the accounts for the same be paid on the certificate of the Judge of the respective District Courts, that in his opinion such accounts are just and reasonable.

Appointment of Deputy Clerk of District Court. SEC. 3. *And the Congress of the Confederate States do further enact,* That any Clerk of any District Court of said Confederate States may, with the consent of such Court, or with the consent in writing of the Judge thereof, in vacation, appoint a deputy, who shall take the

Oath. same oaths such clerk is required to take, and who, during his continu-
Duties. ance in office, may discharge any of the duties of the clerk, and he
Removal from office. may be removed from office either by the Clerk or the Court.

APPROVED April 19, 1862.

April 19, 1862. CHAP. LIII.—*An Act to provide for the payment of officers of the Virginia Militia for services rendered.*

Payment of officers of the Virginia Militia for services rendered the Confederate States. The Congress of the Confederate States of America do enact, That all officers and non-commissioned officers of the Virginia Militia, who have been called into the service of the Confederate States, by the order of any commanding officer of the Confederate States Army, authorized to make such call, or by the proclamation of the Governor of Virginia, in obedience to requisitions duly made upon him by the President, shall be allowed, under the direction of the Quartermaster General, compensation for the period of their actual service, according to the rate of pay and allowances, to which officers and non-commissioned officers of corresponding grades, in the Confederate States Army, are by law entitled.

Officers to produce certificates showing period of service. SEC. 2. Before any officer of militia shall be entitled to receive pay under the provisions of the preceding section, he shall present to the proper officer to whom he may apply for payment, a certificate signed by the commandant of the brigade, regiment or battalion of militia to which he may have been attached, and approved by the Commanding

General of the army, corps or department, with which such brigade, regiment or battalion was serving, which certificate shall state the precise period during which such officer was actually in service and performed duty according to his rank, not including in such period whatever time such officer was absent from duty with his command, unless absent on furlough, or detached or detailed service, by order of the Commanding officer. Non-commissioned officers shall be required to present like certificates, signed by the commanding officer of the regiment or battalion to which they belong, before being entitled to receive their pay.

Sec. 3. All staff officers of the Virginia militia duly appointed and qualified, according to the laws of Virginia, shall be entitled to receive the same pay and allowances as are provided by law for officers of corresponding grades in the Confederate States Army, upon a like certificate that they have actually been in service and performed the duties prescribed for their respective grades by the laws of Virginia, and the laws and army regulations of the Confederate States. *Pay of Staff Officers of the Virginia Militia on like certificates.*

Sec. 4. No payments under this act shall be allowed for any period subsequent to the thirtieth day of March, eighteen hundred and sixty-two, nor shall any junior Major of a regiment to which two Majors may be attached, nor any Paymaster or Surgeon's mate be deemed to be entitled to pay or allowances under the provisions of this act. *No payments to be made for any period subsequent to March 30, 1862.*

Junior Major, Paymaster or Surgeon's mate, to receive no pay.

Approved April 19, 1862.

Chap. LIV.—*An Act to increase the clerical force of the Quartermaster General's Bureau.*   April 19, 1862.

The Congress of the Confederate States of America do enact, That the Secretary of War be, and he is hereby, authorized to appoint eight additional clerks in the Bureau of the Quartermaster General, at the following rates of compensation, to wit: two at the rate of fifteen hundred dollars per annum; two at the rate of twelve hundred dollars per annum; and four at the rate of one thousand dollars per annum: *Provided*, that no person now by law subject to military duty shall be appointed. *Additional clerks authorized in the Bureau of the Quartermaster General.*

Compensation.

Proviso.

Approved April 19, 1862.

Chap. LV.—*An Act to amend An Act entitled "An Act to increase the corps of Artillery, and for other purposes," approved August 21st, 1861.*   April 19, 1862.

The Congress of the Confederate States of America do enact, That section third of an act entitled "An Act to increase the corps of Artillery and for other purposes," approved August 21st, 1861, be so amended as to authorize the President to increase the salaries of master armorers or any of them to a sum not exceeding two thousand dollars per annum. *1861, Aug. 21.*

President may increase salaries of master armorers.

Approved April 19, 1862.

Chap. LVI.—*An Act to amend the several Acts in relation to the pay of Chaplains in the Army.*   April 19, 1862.

The Congress of the Confederate States of America do enact, That hereafter the pay of Chaplains in the army shall be eighty dollars per month, with rations as now provided by law. *Pay of Chaplains.*

Approved April 19, 1862.

April 19, 1862.

    CHAP. LVII.—*An Act to recognize the organization of certain military companies.*

Companies with less than the minimum number, already in the service, recognized as if duly organized.

Rank of the officers.

Pay and rations.

The Congress of the Confederate States of America do enact, That in all cases heretofore occurring where companies not having the minimum number of men necessary to form a company as required by existing laws, have been organized into companies which have entered into the service by order of a Commanding General or been received by such officer into the service, in all such cases the Secretary of War is hereby authorized and required to recognize said companies as if duly organized under existing laws, and the officers of said companies are hereby declared as entitled to the same rank to which they would have been entitled if the companies had been duly organized; and the officers and men thereof shall be entitled to draw their pay and rations as if they had been duly authorized under existing laws.

Approved April 19, 1862.

April 19, 1862.

CHAP. LVIII.—*An Act to prohibit the transportation and sale of certain articles in any port or place within the Confederate States, in the possession of the enemy, and to prohibit the sale, barter or exchange of certain articles therein named, to alien or domestic enemies.*

Unlawful to transport to, or to sell in any port of the U. S. in possession of the enemy, cotton, tobacco, &c.

Penalty.

1861, May 21.

The Congress of the Confederate States of America do enact, That it shall be unlawful for any person, either by himself or his agent, or in any manner whatever, to transport to any port or place in the Confederate States, which may be at the time in the possession of the enemy, or to sell therein, any cotton, tobacco, sugar, rice, molasses, syrup or naval stores.

Sec. 2. *Be it further enacted,* That the provisions of the Act entitled "An Act to prohibit the exportation of cotton from the Confederate States, except through the sea-ports of the said States, and to punish persons offending therein," be and the same are hereby extended to any person or persons violating the foregoing section of this Act, and, in addition to such punishment, the party or parties offending shall forfeit and pay the Confederate States the value of the article sold or transported.

Approved April 19, 1862.

April 19, 1862

CHAP. LIX.—*An Act making Augusta, Georgia, a port of delivery for goods imported into Charleston, South Carolina.*

City of Augusta, Georgia, made a port of delivery for goods imported into Charleston.

The Congress of the Confederate States of America do enact, That from and after the passage of this act, the city of Augusta, Georgia, be, and the same is hereby made a port of delivery for goods imported into Charleston, South Carolina, upon the same terms and conditions, and in like manner, in every respect, as it has been heretofore and is now a port of delivery for goods imported into Savannah, Georgia: and the Secretary of the Treasury is hereby required to make such rules and regulations as may be necessary to carry into effect the true intent and meaning of this act.

Approved April 19, 1862.

April 19, 1862.

CHAP. LX.—*An Act declaring the officer who shall act as President in case of vacancies in the offices both of President and Vice President.*

Who to act as President in case of vacancies in the offices

The Congress of the Confederate States of America do enact, That in case of removal from office, death or resignation both of the President and Vice President of the Confederate States, or of the inability both of President and
Vice President. of both to discharge the powers and duties of the office of President, then the President of the Senate, *pro tempore*, and in case there shall be no President of the Senate, then the Speaker of the House of Representatives, for the time being, shall act as President of the Confederate States, until the disability be removed, or a President shall be elected and inaugurated.

APPROVED April 19, 1862.

CHAP. LXI.—*An Act to authorize the exchange of bonds for articles in kind, and the shipment, sale, or hypotheca ion of such articles.*   April 21, 1862.

The Congress of the Confederate States of America do enact, . That Exchange of bonds
or stocks for articles
in kind. the Secretary of the Treasury be, and he is hereby authorized to exchange the bonds or stock of the Confederate States for any articles in kind, which may be required for the use of the Government, the said articles to be valued according to such regulations as the said Secretary shall make. Articles to be valued.

SEC. 2. It shall be the duty of the Commissary and Quartermaster Generals to direct their various officers to receive, at the place of purchase, all such articles purchased as are applicable to their several Departments, and to apply the same in the same manner as if purchased directly by themselves; and the officer to whom each article is delivered shall be charged with the value as declared by the purchase, and shall be bound to account for the same. Receipt of articles
at the place of pur-
chase, how to be ap-
plied.
Officers charged
with their value.

SEC. 3. The said Secretary is also authorized to accept for the use of Exchange of bonds
or stock for cotton,
tobacco, etc., sub-
scribed to the Pro-
duce Loan the Government in exchange for the said bonds or stock, cotton, tobacco, and other agricultural products in kind, which have been subscribed to the Produce Loan, or which may be subscribed in kind at such rates as may be adjusted between the parties and the agents of the Government : *Provided*, That in no event shall he receive of cotton or tobacco, a greater value than thirty-five millions of dollars; and the said Proviso. Secretary is further authorized to deposit the same at such places as Power given Secre-
tary of the Treasury
over articles received
in exchange. he shall deem proper, and to procure advances thereon by hypothecation, or to ship the same abroad, or to sell the same at home or abroad, as he may deem best; and, to assist these operations, the said Secretary may issue Produce Certificates, which shall entitle the party to whom May issue Produce
Certificates; their ef-
fect. issued, or his endorsee, to receive the produce therein set forth, and to ship the same to any neutral port, in conformity with the laws of the Confederate States.

SEC. 4. The Secretary of the Treasury may, from time to time, appoint and dismiss such agents as he may deem requisite to carry into effect the provisions of this act. Their compensation shall be a brokerage upon the business completed by them at such rates as the Secretary of the Treasury shall adjust by general regulation. May appoint and
dismiss agents.
Compensation of
agents.

SEC 5. The Secretary of the Treasury may, from time to time, issue regulations for carrying out all the details involved in the provisions of this act, which shall be obligatory upon all parties concerned therein. Regulations to car-
ry out the details of
this act.

APPROVED April 21, 1862.

CHAP. LXII.—*An Act to punish drunkenness in the Army.*   April 21, 1862.

The Congress of the Confederate States of America do enact, That Punishment for
drunkenness of com-
missioned officers in
the Army. any commissioned officer of the Regular or Provisional Army who shall be found drunk, either while on or off duty, shall, on conviction thereof before a court of inquiry, be cashiered or suspended from the service of the Confederate States, or be publicly reprimanded, according to the aggravation of the offence, and in addition to a sentence cashiering any such officer, he may also be declared incapable of holding any military office under the Confederate States during the war.

Duty of all officers to make report thereof.

SEC. 2. That it shall be the duty of all officers to report to the commanding officer of the post, regiment or corps to which they belong, all cases coming under their observation of intoxication of commissioned officers, whether of superior or inferior grades to themselves; and it shall be the duty of the commanding officer of the division or brigade to which said post, regiment or corps belongs, to whom such report may be made, to report the same to the officer commanding the

Court for the trial of offenders.

brigade or division, who shall organize said court and order the trial of said offender at the earliest time consistent with the public service.

Findings of the Court.

SEC. 3. The findings of any such court shall be promptly transmitted to the Secretary of War, by the commanding officer, together with his approval or disapproval thereof, and shall be reported to Congress at the next session thereafter, by the said Secretary.

APPROVED April 21, 1862.

April 21, 1862.

CHAP. LXIII.—*An Act to organize bands of Partisan Rangers.*

Bands of Partisan Rangers.

The Congress of the Confederate States of America do enact, That the President be and he is hereby authorized to commission such officers as he may deem proper with authority to form bands of Partisan Rangers, in companies, battalions or regiments, either as infantry or cavalry, the companies, battalions or regiments to be composed each of such numbers as the President may approve.

Pay, rations and quarters.

SEC. 2. *Be it further enacted*, That such Partisan Rangers, after being regularly received into service, shall be entitled to the same pay, rations and quarters during their term of service, and be subject to the same regulations as other soldiers.

The Rangers entitled to full value of the arms, etc., captured.

SEC. 3. *Be it further enacted*, That for any arms and munitions of war captured from the enemy by any body of Partisan Rangers and delivered to any Quartermaster at such place or places as may be designated by a Commanding General, the Rangers shall be paid their full value in such manner as the Secretary of War may prescribe.

APPROVED April 21, 1862.

April 21, 1862.

CHAP. LXIV.—*A Bill [An Act] for the enlistment of Cooks in the Army.*

Enlistment of Cooks in the Army.

The Congress of the Confederate States of America do enact, That hereafter it shall be duty of the Captain or Commanding Officer of his

Their duties.

company to enlist four Cooks for the use of his company, whose duty it shall be to cook for such company—taking charge of the supplies, utensils and other things furnished therefor, and safely keep the same, subject to such rules and regulations as may be prescribed by the War Department or the Colonel of the Regiment to which such company may be attached:

May be white or black, free or slave persons.

[SEC. 2.] *Be it further enacted*, That the Cooks so directed to be enlisted, may be white or black, free or slave persons: *Provided, however*, That no slave shall be so enlisted, without the written consent of

Proviso.

his owner. And such Cooks shall be enlisted as such only, and put on the muster-roll and paid at the time and place the company may or shall be paid off, twenty dollars per month to the Chief or Head Cook,

and fifteen dollars per month for each of the Assistant Cooks, together
with the same allowance for clothing, or the same commutation therefor that may be allowed to the rank and file of the company.

Approved April 21, 1862.

Pay and allowances.

CHAP. LXV.—*An Act to increase the corps of Engineers of the Provisional Army.*   April 21, 1862.

The Congress of the Confederate States of America do enact, That
the President be and he is hereby authorized to appoint with the advice and consent of the Senate, an additional number of officers in the
Engineer Corps of the Provisional Army, of a rank not higher than
Captain: *Provided,* That the whole Corps shall not exceed one hundred.

Approved April 21, 1862.

Appointment of additional officers in the Engineer Corps of Provisional Army.

Rank.
Number.

CHAP. LXVI.—*An Act to authorise the appointment of officers of Artillery in the Provisional Army.*   April 21, 1862.

The Congress of the Confederate States of America do enact, That
for the purpose of enlarging the number of officers of Artillery, and
enabling them to discharge more effectually the duties of Ordnance
officers, the President is hereby authorized to appoint, with the advice
and consent of the Senate, officers of Artillery, of the rank of Captain
and First Lieutenant, in the Provisional Army, not exceeding eighty
in number.

Approved April 21, 1862.

Appointment of officers of Artillery in the Provisional Army.

Rank.
Number.

CHAP. LXVII.—*An Act regulating the compensation of deputy Post Masters.*   April 21, 1862.

The Congress of the Confederate States of America do enact, That
from and after the first day of July next, the Deputy Post Masters of
the Confederate States be allowed the following commissions and none
other for their compensation, respectively, viz: On any sum not exceeding one hundred dollars, fifty per cent., except such Deputy Post Masters as regularly receive the mail at their offices between the hours of
nine o'clock at night and five o'clock in the morning, who shall be entitled to sixty per cent., on the amount received as postage under one
hundred dollars. On all sums over one hundred dollars received as
postage, and not exceeding four hundred dollars, forty per cent. On all
sums so received, over four hundred dollars, and not exceeding twenty-four hundred dollars, thirty per cent., and on all sums over twenty-
four hundred dollars, ten per cent. Deputy Post Masters at distributing offices shall receive eight per cent. commission on the amount of
postage on letters and packages received at such distributing offices,
respectively, for distribution; which said several commissions shall be
allowed quarterly and in due proportion for any period less than a quar-
ter, but these commissions shall in no case exceed the maximum compensation now allowed by law.

Approved April 21, 1862.

Commissions allowed Deputy Postmasters.

4

April 21, 1862. Chap. LXVIII.—*An Act to amend An Act entitled "An Act to provide for the organization of the Navy, approved March 16, 1861, and for other purposes."*

1661, March 16.

Grades of the Commissioned officers of the Navy.

The Congress of the Confederate States of America do enact, That the grades of the commissioned officers of the Navy of the Confederate States shall hereafter be as follows, to wit: four Admirals, ten Captains, thirty-one Commanders, one hundred First Lieutenants, twenty-five Second Lieutenants, twenty Masters in line of promotion, twelve Paymasters, forty Assistant Paymasters, twenty-two Surgeons, fifteen Past Assistant Surgeons, thirty Assistant Surgeons, one Engineer-in-Chief and twelve Engineers.

Officers appointed only for gallant or meritorious conduct.

Appointments; how made.
Service to be specified in the Commission.
Proviso.

SEC. 2. All the Admirals, four of the Captains, five of the Commanders, twenty-two of the First Lieutenants, and five of the Second Lieutenants, shall be appointed solely for gallant or meritorious conduct during the war. The appointments shall be made from the grade immediately below the one to be filled and without reference to the rank of the officer in such grade, and the service for which the appointment shall be conferred shall be specified in the commission: *Provided,* That all officers below the grade of Second Lieutenant may be promoted more than one grade for the same service.

Warrant officers.

SEC. 3. The Warrant Officers shall be as follows: twenty Passed Midshipmen, one hundred and six Acting Midshipmen, fifty First Assistant Engineers, one hundred and fifty Second Assistant Engineers, one hundred and fifty Third Assistant Engineers, ten Boatswains, twenty Gunners, six Sail Makers and twenty Carpenters.

Pay of the additional grades.

SEC. 4. The annual pay of the additional grades created by this act shall be as follows: Admirals, six thousand dollars; Second Lieutenant, for service afloat, twelve hundred dollars; when on leave or other duty, one thousand dollars; Master in the line of promotion, one thousand dollars for service afloat; when on leave or other duty, nine hundred dollars; Past Midshipmen, nine hundred dollars for services afloat; when on leave or other duty, eight hundred dollars.

Pay of Assistant Paymasters.

SEC. 5. The annual pay of Assistant Paymasters shall hereafter be when on service afloat, twelve hundred dollars; on other duty, eleven hundred dollars.

APPROVED April 21, 1862.

April 21, 1862. Chap. LXIX.—*An Act making appropriations to carry into effect "An Act authorizing the exchange of bonds for articles in kind, and the shipment, sale or hypothecation of such articles."*

Appropriation to carry into effect the act authorizing the exchange of bonds for articles in kind.

The Congress of the Confederate States of America do enact, That for the purpose of carrying into effect an act authorizing the exchange of Bonds for articles in kind, and the shipment, sale, or hypothecation of such articles, the sum of two millions of dollars is hereby appropriated.

APPROVED April 21, 1862.

April 21, 1862. Chap. LXX.—*An Act to increase the facilities of importing goods, wares and merchandise into the ports of the Confederate States.*

Vessels may unload their cargoes on any part of the coast.

Laws suspended.

The Congress of the Confederate States of America do enact, That it shall be lawful for vessels to unload their cargoes on any part of the coast of the Confederate States, and that the laws requiring entry of vessels or discharge of their cargoes at designated ports, and prescribing penalties for failure to do so, shall be, and the same are hereby suspended.

APPROVED April 21, 1862.

CHAP. LXXI.—*An Act to amend An Act entitled " An Act to amend An Act recognizing the existence of war between the United States and the Confederate States, and concerning letters of Marque, prizes and prize goods," approved May 21st, 1861.*   April 21, 1862.

The Congress of the Confederate States of America do enact, That the first section of the above entitled Act be so amended, that, in case any person or persons shall invent or construct any new machine or engine, or contrive any new method for destroying the armed vessels of the enemy, he or they shall receive fifty per centum of the value of each and every such vessel that may be sunk or destroyed, by means of such invention or contrivance, including the value of the armament thereof, in lieu of twenty per centum, as provided by said Act.

Act of 1861, May 21, §1, amended.

Inventors or constructors of machines for destroying the armed vessels of the enemy; their compensation.

APPROVED April 21, 1862.

CHAP. LXXII.—*An Act to organize Battalions of Sharp Shooters.*   /   April 21, 1862.

The Congress of the Confederate States of America do enact, That the Secretary of War may cause to be organized a battalion of sharp shooters for each brigade, consisting of not less than three nor more than six companies, to be composed of men selected from the brigade or otherwise, and armed with long range muskets or rifles, said companies to be organized, and the commissioned officers therefor appointed by the President, by and with the advice, and consent of the Senate. Such battalion shall constitute parts of the brigades to which they belong, and shall have such field and staff officers as are authorized by law for similar battalions, to be appointed by the President, by and with the advice and consent of the Senate.

Battalions of sharp shooters.

How to be armed.

Commissioned officers appointed by the President.

Also field and staff officers.

SEC. 2. *Be it further enacted,* That for the purpose of arming the said battalion, the long range muskets and rifles in the hands of the troops, may be taken for that purpose: *Provided,* the Government has not at its command a sufficient number of approved long range rifles or muskets, wherewith to arm said corps.

May be armed with long range muskets, etc., in the hands of troops.

Proviso.

APPROVED April 21, 1862.

CHAP. LXXIII.—*An Act supplementary to An Act further to provide for the Public Defence.*   April 21, 1862.

The Congress of the Confederate States of America do enact, That the President be and he is hereby authorized, to accept the services of any companies, squadrons, battalions or regiments which have been organized and are now in service under the authority of any of the States of the Confederacy, and which may be tendered by the Governors of said States, with an organization conforming to the Act of March Sixth, A. D. eighteen hundred and sixty-one, " to provide for the public defence."

President authorised to accept the services of companies, etc., now in service under State authority.

1861, March 6.

APPROVED April 21, 1862.

CHAP. LXXIV.—*An Act to exempt certain persons from enrollment for service in the Armies of the Confederate States.*   April 21, 1862.

The Congress of the Confederate States of America do enact, That all persons who shall be held to be unfit for military services under rules to be prescribed by the Secretary of War; all in the service or employ of the Confederate States; all judicial and executive officers of Confederate or State Governments; the members of both Houses of the Congress and of the Legislatures of the several States and their respective officers; all clerks of the officers of the State and Confederate Governments allowed by law; all engaged in car-

Persons exempted from military service.

rying the mails; all ferrymen on post routes; all pilots and persons engaged in the marine service and in. actual service on river and railroad routes of transportation; telegraphic operators, and ministers of religion in the regular discharge of ministerial duties; all engaged in working iron mines, furnaces and foundries; all journeymen printers actually employed in printing newspapers; all presidents and professors of colleges and academies, and all teachers having as many as twenty scholars; superintendents of the public hospitals, lunatic asylums and the regular nurses and attendants therein, and the teachers employed in the institution for the deaf and dumb, and blind: in each apothecary store now established and doing business, one apothecary in good standing who is a practical druggist; superintendents and operatives in wool and cotton factories, who may be exempted by the Secretary of War;—shall be and are. hereby exempted from military service in the armies of the Confederate States. ·

APPROVED April 21, 1862.

April 21, 1862.

1862, April 16.

CHAP. LXXV.—*An Act to amend An Act entitled An Act to further provide for the public defence, passed the sixteenth day of April, eighteen hundred and sixty-two.*

Vacancies in companies, battalions, etc., filled by promotion according to seniority.

Vacancy in the lowest grade of commissioned officers of a company filled by election.

President may fill vacancies by the promotion of officers or privates for distinguished services.

The Congress of the Confederate States of America do enact, That all vacancies shall be filled by the President from the company, battalion, squadron or regiment in which such vacancies shall occur, by promotion, according to seniority, except in case of disability or other incompetency, and that whenever a vacancy shall occur in the lowest grade of commissioned officers of a company, such vacancies shall be filled by election: *Provided, however,* That the President may, when in his opinion it is proper, fill any vacancy by the promotion of any officer from any company, battalion, squadron or regiment in which the same may occur, who shall have been distinguished in service by the exhibition of extraordinary valor and skill; and that when any vacancy shall occur in the lowest grade of commissioned officers of any company, the same may be filled by selection by the President of any noncommissioned officer or private from the company in which said vacancy may occur, who shall have been distinguished in the service by the exhibition of extraordinary valor and skill; and that appointments made by the President shall be by and with the advice and consent of the Senate.

APPROVED April 21, 1862.

RESOLUTIONS.

[No. 1.] *Joint resolution approving the resolution passed by the Legislature of Virginia expressing her determination to vindicate her ancient boundaries.* February 27, 1862.

Resolved by the Senate and House of Representatives of the Confederate States of America, That they heartily approve of the resolution passed by the Legislature of Virginia, expressing her determination to vindicate the integrity of her ancient boundaries, and pledge all the resources of the Confederacy to uphold her determination.
APPROVED Feb. 27, 1862.

Approval of Resolution passed by the Legislature of Virginia.

[No. 2.] *A Resolution declaring the sense of Congress in regard to re-uniting with the United States.* March 11, 1862.

Whereas the United States are waging war against the Confederate States, with the avowed purpose of compelling the latter to reunite with them under the same Constitution and Government; and whereas the waging of war with such an object is in direct opposition to the sound republican maxim, that "all government rests upon the consent of the governed," and can only tend to consolidation in the General Government, and the consequent destruction of the rights of the States; and whereas this result being attained, the two sections can only exist together in the relation of the oppressor and the oppressed, because of the great preponderance of power in the Northern section, coupled with dissimilarity of interest; and whereas we, the representatives of the people of the Confederate States, in Congress, assembled, may be presumed to know the sentiments of said people, having just been elected by them: Therefore—

Preamble.

Be it resolved by the Congress of the Confederate States of America, That this Congress do solemnly declare and publish to the world, that it is the unalterable determination of the people of the Confederate States, in humble reliance upon Almighty God, to suffer all the calamities of the most protracted war, but that they will never, on any terms, politically affiliate with a people who are guilty of an invasion of their soil and the butchery of their citizens.
APPROVED March 11, 1862.

No political affiliation with the people of the United States.

[No. 3.] *Resolution pledging the Government to maintain the territorial integrity of the Confederacy.* March 11, 1862.

Resolved by the Congress of the Confederate States of America, That the honor of this Government imperatively demands that the existing war be prosecuted until the enemy shall have been expelled from every foot of soil within each and every of the Confederate States; and no proposition of peace shall be entertained which contemplates, however remotely, the relinquishment, by this Government, of any portion of any of the States of this Confederacy.
APPROVED March 11, 1862.

The territorial integrity of the Confederacy, to be maintained.

[No. 4.] *Resolution of thanks to Capt. Buchanan and the officers and men under his command.* March 12, 1862.

Resolved by the Congress of the Confederate States of America, That the thanks of Congress are due and are hereby cordially tendered to Captain Buchanan, and all under his command, for their unsurpassed gallantry, as displayed in the recent successful attack upon the naval forces of the enemy in Hampton Roads.
APPROVED March 12, 1862.

Thanks of Congress to Capt. Buchanan and his command.

March 25, 1862.   [No. 5.] *Joint resolution to aid our prisoners in the hands of the enemy.*

Aid to our prison-
ers of war in the
hands of the enemy.

Resolved by the Congress of the Confederate States of America,
That the Secretary of War be authorized to apply out of the contingent fund of the War Department, such sums of money, from time to
time, as, in his judgment, may be necessary for the aid of prisoners of
Proviso. war in the hands of the enemy : *Provided,* That all sums paid any prisoner, or expended for him, shall be charged to his account.
APPROVED March 25, 1862.

April 3, 1862.   [No. 6.] *Joint resolution relating to the manner of paying Members of the Provisional Congress
the arrearages of their pay and mileage.*

Manner of paying
members of the Pro-
visional Congress
the arrearages of
their pay and mileage.

Resolved by the Congress of the Confederate States of America,
That the pay and mileage of members of the Provisional Congress,
who have not been paid may be paid upon certificates signed by the
Speaker of the House of Representatives, on the recommendation of
the House Committee on pay and mileage, out of any money appropriated for that purpose.
APPROVED April 3, 1862.

April 9, 1862.   [No. 7.] *Resolutions of thanks to Major General Thomas J. Jackson and the officers and men under
his command, for gallant and meritorious services in the battle of Kernstown.*

Thanks of Congress
to Major-Gen. Jack-
son and his command.

Resolved by the Congress of the Confederate States of America,
That the thanks of Congress are due and are hereby tendered to Major-
General Thomas J. Jackson and the officers and men under his command for gallant and meritorious services in a successful engagement
with a greatly superior force of the enemy near Kernstown, Frederick
County, Virginia, on the twenty-third day of March, eighteen hundred
and sixty-two.

Secretary of War
to communicate these
resolutions.

Resolved, That these resolutions be communicated by the Secretary
of War to Major-General Jackson, and by him, to his command.
APPROVED April 9, 1862.

April 11, 1862.   [No. 8.] *Joint resolution of thanks to the patriotic women of the country for voluntary contributions
furnished by them to the Army.*

Thanks of Congress
to the patriotic women
of the country.

Resolved by the Congress of the Confederate States of America,
That the thanks of the Congress of the Confederate States are emi-
nently due, and are hereby tendered to the patriotic women of the
Confederacy for the energy, zeal and untiring devotion which they have
manifested in furnishing voluntary contributions to our soldiers in the
field, and in the various military hospitals throughout the country.
APPROVED April 11, 1862.

April 15, 1862.   [No. 9.] *Joint resolution of thanks for the victory at Shiloh, Tenn.*

Gratitude of Con-
gress for the victory
achieved at Shiloh.

Resolved by the Congress of the Confederate States of America,
That Congress has learned with gratitude to the Divine Ruler of nations the intelligence of the recent complete and brilliant victory which
has been gained by the Army of the Confederate States under the command of Gen. A. S. Johnston, over the Federal forces in Tennessee, on
the battle field of Shiloh.

Resolved, That the thanks of Congress are hereby tendered to Gen. G. T. Beauregard and the other surviving officers and privates of that army for the signal exhibition of skill and gallantry displayed by them on that memorable occasion; and all who contributed to that signal triumph, in the judgment of Congress, are entitled to the gratitude of their country.

Thanks of Congress to Gen. Beauregard and other surviving officers and privates.

Resolved, That the intelligence of the death of General Albert Sidney Johnston, Commander-in-Chief, when leading the Confederate forces to victory on the sixth of April, in Tennessee, while it affects Congress with profound sorrow, at the same time obscures our joy with a shade of sadness at the loss of an officer, so able, skillful and gallant.

Sorrow of Congress occasioned by the intelligence of the death of Gen. Johnston.

Resolved, That the foregoing resolutions be made known by appropriate general orders by the Generals in command, to the officers and troops to whom they are addressed, and that they also be communicated to the family of General Johnston.

These resolutions to be made known to the officers, etc., to whom addressed.

Approved April 15, 1862.

[No. 10.] *Joint resolution of thanks to General H. H. Sibley and his command.*   April 16, 1862.

Resolved by the Congress of the Confederate States of America, That the thanks of Congress are hereby tendered to Brig. Gen. H. H. Sibley, and to the officers and men under his command, for the complete and brilliant victories achieved over our enemies in New Mexico.

Thanks of Congress to Brig.-Gen. Sibley and his command.

Approved April 16, 1862.

[No. 11.] *Resolution of thanks to the officers and crews of the Patrick Henry, Jamestown, Teazer and other vessels for gallant conduct.*   April 16, 1862.

Resolved by the Congress of the Confederate States of America, That the thanks of Congress are due, and are hereby tendered to the officers and crews of the Patrick Henry, Jamestown, Teazer and other vessels engaged, for their gallant conduct and bearing in the naval combat and brilliant victory on the waters of James river, on the 8th and 9th of March, 1862.

Thanks of Congress to the officers and crews of the Patrick Henry, Jamestown, Teazer and other vessels.

Approved April 16, 1862.

[No. 12.] *Resolution for the preservation of public documents.*   April 19, 1862.

Resolved by the Congress of the Confederate States of America, That two hundred copies of all documents printed by order of either House of Congress shall be delivered by the Superintendent of Public Printing to the Attorney General, and at the end of each session of Congress, the Attorney General shall cause the same to be properly indexed and bound in volumes of convenient size, including in each volume one copy of each document; but no document from which the seal of secresy has not been removed shall be placed in said bound volumes.

Preservation of documents printed by order of either House of Congress.

To be indexed and bound.

Resolved further, That one copy of said volumes, when bound, shall be retained for the use of the Department of Justice, and the remaining copies together with the secret documents, held subject to the order of Congress.

How disposed of.

Approved April 19, 1862.

April 19, 1862.　[No. 13.] *Joint Resolution to authorize the Secretary of the Treasury to pay the mileage and per diem of members of the Provisional Congress out of the contingent fund of that Congress.*

Contingent fund of the Provisional Congress to be used in paying its members their mileage and per diem.

Resolved by the Congress of the Confederate States of America, That the Secretary of the Treasury be, and he is hereby authorized to use the fund appropriated by the Provisional Congress for contingencies for that Congress, in paying members of the Provisional Congress, who have not already been paid the mileage and per diem due them.
APPROVED April 19, 1862.

April 21, 1862·　[No. 14.] *Resolution of thanks to Major Generals Van Dorn and Price, and the officers and soldiers under their command, for their valour, skill and good conduct, in the battle of Elk Horn, in the State of Arkansas, and of respect for the memory of Generals McCulloch and McIntosh.*

Thanks of Congress to Major Generals Van Dorn and Price and their respective commands.

Resolved by the Congress of the Confederate States of America, That the thanks of Congress be, and they are hereby given to Major-Generals Van Dorn and Price, and the officers and soldiers under their command, for their valor, skill and good conduct in the battle of 'Elkhorn, in the State of Arkansas.

Grief of Congress at the death of Generals McCulloch and McIntosh.

Resolved, further, That the Congress has heard with profound grief, of the deaths of Generals McCulloch and McIntosh, who fell in the midst of the battle, gloriously leading their commands against the enemy.
APPROVED April 21, 1862.

April 21, 1862.　[No. 15.] *Joint Resolution to provide for the payment of stationery purchased for the Provisional Congress.*

Account of Starke and Cardoza for stationery.

Resolved by the Congress of the Confederate States of America, That the clerk of the House of Representatives is hereby authorized to pay out of the contingent fund of the Provisional Congress, the account of Starke and Cardoza, for the sum of ten hundred and forty-five dollars and sixty cents, for stationery furnished the Provisional Congress.
APPROVED April 21, 1862.

April 21, 1862.　[No. 16.] *Joint Resolution to authorize the joint committee on public buildings to rent rooms for the Treasury Department.*

Rent of additional rooms for the use of the Treasury Department.

Resolved by the Congress of the Confederate States of America, That the Joint Committee on Public Buildings be authorized to rent as many additional rooms as may be necessary for the use of the Treasury Department.
APPROVED April 21, 1862.

INDEX

FOREGOING PUBLIC LAWS AND RESOLUTIONS

OF THE CONFEDERATE STATES.

Q.

R.

PRIVATE LAWS

OF THE

CONFEDERATE STATES OF AMERICA,

PASSED AT THE FIRST SESSION

OF THE

FIRST CONGRESS;

1862.

𝔆arefully collated with the 𝔒riginals at 𝔕ichmond.

EDITED BY

JAMES M. MATTHEWS,

ATTORNEY AT LAW,

AND LAW CLERK IN THE DEPARTMENT OF JUSTICE.

TO BE CONTINUED ANNUALLY.

RICHMOND:

R. M. SMITH, PRINTER TO CONGRESS.

1862.

ADVERTISEMENT.

CONFEDERATE STATES OF AMERICA,
Department of Justice,
Richmond, June 1, 1862.

By an Act of the Provisional Congress, approved on the 5th day of August, 1861, section third, it was made, *inter alia,* "the duty of the Attorney General, at the close of each session of Congress, to cause all the laws and resolutions having the force of laws, and all treaties entered into by the Confederate States, to be published under the supervision of the Superintendent of Public Printing." This section was amended by a further act, approved on the 17th day of February, 1862, which provides, "That the third section of said act be so amended as to authorise the Attorney General to cause three thousand copies of the Provisional and Permanent Constitution, and of all the acts and resolutions and treaties of the Provisional Government of the Confederate States which are not secret, to be published in one volume, at the close of the present session of Congress, arranged, and with marginal notes, and indexed, as provided in said act." The effect of this amendment, it will be observed, is to repeal the third section of the first mentioned act, so far as it applies to the legislation of the Provisional Congress, and restrict its application to the laws and resolutions passed by Congress under the Permanent Constitution, and to treaties entered into by the Confederate States under that Constitution.

For sometime after the passage of the act of the 5th day of August last, it was impossible to comply with its requirements because of the fact that the requisite paper—"paper equal in quality to the edition of the laws of the United States, as annually published by Little & Brown,"—could not be procured; and it was not till very recently that the Superintendent of Public Printing succeeded in obtaining it. For this reason the laws and resolutions have been published, heretofore, under special resolutions of Congress, for temporary convenience, on paper of inferior quality, and without regard to the provisions of the act. This is the first publication that has been made in conformity with its provisions.

The following laws and resolutions have been carefully compared with the original Rolls on file in this Department, and all typographical errors other than those noted in the table of errata, corrected. Where anything essential to complete the sense is omitted in the Rolls it is inserted in the text, included in brackets.

JAMES M. MATTHEWS,
Law Clerk.

LIST

OF THE

PRIVATE ACTS AND RESOLUTIONS

OF CONGRESS.

Acts of the First Congress of the Confederate States.

STATUTE I.—1862.

PRIVATE RESOLUTIONS.

PRIVATE ACTS OF THE FIRST CONGRESS

OF THE

CONFEDERATE STATES.

Passed at the first session, which was begun and held at the City of Richmond, in the State of Virginia, on Tuesday, the eighteenth day of February, A. D , 1862, and ended on Monday, the twenty-first day of April, A. D., 1862.

JEFFERSON DAVIS, President. ALEXANDER H. STEPHENS, Vice President, and President of the Senate. THOMAS S. BOCOCK, Speaker of the House of Representatives.

CHAP. I.—*An Act for the relief of Mrs. Caroline Miller and her children.* April 17, 1862.

WHEREAS, Mrs. Caroline Miller, wife of James H. Miller, a soldier now in the Confederate Army, is in very indigent circumstances; and whereas, her brother, one John A. Bridgeland, a resident of the State of Indiana, in the month of September, in the year of our Lord, one thousand eight hundred and fifty-seven, purchased a house and lot in the town of Salem, in the county of Roanoke, in the State of Virginia, known in the Plan of said town as Lot No. 81, declaring at the time of receiving a deed for the same in his own name, that he was buying the said property for the use and benefit of the said Caroline Miller and her children; and whereas, proceedings are now pending in the District Court of the Confederate States, in and for the Western District of Virginia, to subject the said house and lot to sequestration, by virtue of the act of the Provisional Congress of the said Confederate States, entitled "An Act for the sequestration of the estates, property and effects of alien enemies, and for the indemnity of citizens of the Confederate States, and persons aiding the same in the existing war with the United States," approved August the 30th, 1861—Therefore, *[Preamble.]*

The Congress of the Confederate States of America do enact, That whenever a judgment or decree of sequestration shall be rendered in the District Court for the Western District of Virginia, subjecting the above described house and lot, of the said John A. Bridgeland to sequestration, it shall be the duty of the receiver of the District in which said property is situated, instead of selling the same, to convey it to such person as shall be designated by the said Court, to be held in trust for the sole and separate use and benefit of the said Caroline Miller, during her life, and, after her death, for the children and their heirs, so as not to be liable to the debts or contracts of her husband, James H. Miller, which said conveyance shall have the effect of passing to the said trustee, for the use aforesaid, the title of the said John A. Bridgeland. *[House and lot to be conveyed in trust for Caroline Miller and her children,]*

SEC. 2. *Be it further enacted,* That the said Caroline Miller is hereby discharged from all liability, under the Sequestration Act, for the *[discharged from all liabilities.]*

6

rents and profits of the house and lot, now due, or hereafter accruing, and that she shall be permitted to remain in the use and occupation of the same until the conveyance shall be made for her benefit, according to the provisions of this act, any order, judgment or decree of the said District Court to the contrary notwithstanding.

Commencement of act.

Sec. 3. *Be it further enacted,* That this act shall be in force from and after its ratification.

Approved April 17, 1862.

April 19, 1862.   Chap. II.—*An Act for the relief of the legal representative of Samuel M. Wilkes, late Adjutant of the Fourth Regiment, South Carolina Volunteers.*

The legal representatives of Samuel M. Wilkes, deceased, to be paid arrearages, etc., due decedent,

The Congress of the Confederate States of America do enact, That the Secretary of the Treasury be, and he is hereby directed to pay to the legal representatives of Samuel M. Wilkes, late Adjutant of the Fourth South Carolina Regiment of Volunteers, out of any money in the Treasury not otherwise appropriated, one hundred and fifty dollars arrearages due him from the sixth day of June to the twenty-first day *and for his horse killed in battle.* of July, eighteen hundred and sixty-one, and also the sum of one hundred and sixty dollars for his horse which was killed in the battle of Manassas.

Approved April 19, 1862.

RESOLUTIONS.

March 25, 1862.   [No. 1.] *A joint resolution providing for the payment to Mrs. Julia Tyler of the arrearages of pay due to Hon. John Tyler, deceased, for services in the Provisional Congress.*

Pay and mileage due the Hon. John Tyler, deceased, as a member of the Provisional Congress to be paid to his legal representative.

Resolved by the Congress of the Confederate States of America, That the Committee on pay and mileage of the House of Representatives be authorized and required to ascertain, at the Treasury, the amount of pay and mileage due to the Hon. John Tyler, deceased, at the time of his death, for services as a member of the Provisional Congress; and to pay the amount so ascertained to be due, to Mrs. Julia Tyler, the legal representative of said deceased.

Approved March 25, 1862.

April 19, 1862.   [No. 2.] *Joint Resolution for the relief of Capt. Ben Desha.*

The accounts of Captain Ben Desha for transportation of his company, to be adjusted and paid.

Resolved by the Congress of the Confederate States of America, That the Quartermaster General be and is hereby authorized to audit and adjust the accounts of Captain Ben Desha, of the Fifth Regiment of Kentucky Volunteers, for expenses incurred by him for the transportation of his company from Cynthiana, Kentucky, to Abingdon, Virginia, being the first place at which said company could be mustered into service, and to pay him whatever amount may be ascertained to be due him on account of such transportation; said company having been organized within the lines of the enemy.

Approved April 19, 1862.

INDEX

TO THE

FOREGOING PRIVATE LAWS AND RESOLUTIONS.

———————

CPSIA information can be obtained
at www.ICGtesting.com
Printed in the USA
LVHW04s1433260918
591442LV00009B/589/P